MOTIVATED

Ilana Seidel Horn

Designing **Math Classrooms** Where Students Want to **Join In**

MOTIVATED

Heinemann • Portsmouth NH

Heinemann
361 Hanover Street
Portsmouth, NH 03801–3912
www.heinemann.com

Offices and agents throughout the world

The author and publisher wish to thank those who have generously given permission to reprint borrowed material:

Visual Patterns 1, 84, and 153 from www.visualpatterns.org. Copyright © 2017 by Fawn Nguyen. Reprinted by permission.

Excerpt from "Güerita" blog post by Anne Schwartz, November 3, 2016. https://abrandnewline.wordpress.com/2016/11/03/guerita/. Reprinted by permission.

Slides from "Pick a Point" PowerPoint by Dan Meyer, Chief Academic Officer at Desmos. The 2016 CMC Sessions, http://cmc16.mrmeyer.com/2015/02/13/math-is-power-not-punishment/. Reprinted by permission.

Low Floor/High Ceiling Questions adapted from "Create Debate" by Will Stafford. NCTM San Francisco 2016 Session, https://nctm.confex.com/nctm/2016AM/webprogram/Session41215.html. Reprinted by permission.

Library of Congress Cataloging-in-Publication Data
Names: Horn, Ilana Seidel, author.
Title: Motivated : designing math classrooms where students want to join in /
    Ilana Seidel Horn.
Description: Portsmouth, NH : Heinemann, [2017]
Identifiers: LCCN 2017009951 | ISBN 9780325089812
Subjects: LCSH: Mathematics—Study and teaching. | Motivation in education. |
    Effective teaching.
Classification: LCC QA11.2 .H65 2017 | DDC 510.71—dc23
LC record available at https://lccn.loc.gov/2017009951

Editor: Katherine Bryant
Production Editor: Sonja S. Chapman
Typesetter: Kim Arney
Cover and interior design: Suzanne Heiser
Manufacturing: Steve Bernier

Printed in the United States of America on acid-free paper
21 20 19 18 17   ML   1 2 3 4 5

This book is dedicated to
Peg Cagle, Rafranz Davis, Sadie Estrella,
Chris Luzniak, Fawn Nguyen, Elizabeth Statmore,
and all of the dedicated mathematics
teachers who show me what is possible with their
intelligence, insight, imagination, and love.

CONTENTS

FOREWORD

The book you're holding will help you resolve a paradox of mathematics instruction: your students are chatty and irrepressible *outside* of your classroom and yet when asked to chat mathematically *inside* your classroom, they're silent and repressed. How are these the same students?

It isn't easy to live in that paradox. Many educators have made their escape by deciding that mathematics is a quiet discipline, that mathematics requires focused, interior work that other disciplines, and certainly that your students' lives outside your classroom, simply do not.

You're here because you believe otherwise. Perhaps that's because you witnessed a moment where one of your student's two identities merged into one and for a brief interval she was as animated *inside* your class about a mathematical idea as she is *outside* your class about weekend plans. You may have thought such moments were incomprehensible and isolated. Lani Horn's book will help you understand and multiply these moments.

You will be disappointed to come to the end of this book. From there you may find yourself on one of two paths.

On one path, you'll do your best to put into practice everything you've learned from this book. You'll experience frequent successes and intermittent failures and whether your practice ultimately converges on success or failure will depend largely on your own insight and industry. I have walked this path and found it lonely. It is possible to walk quickly along it, but not *far.*

On the other path, you'll realize that this book has its genesis in a particular community of math educators, a community that takes physical shape on rare occasions in pubs and conference halls but that otherwise exists exclusively on the Internet. It's in that community where I first met Lani. That community is where she assembled the cast of teachers who populate this book with their ideas.

That community is available to you as well.

The authors and featured teachers in books like this often seem remote, separated from you by their titles, degrees, and profound ideas. But the only separation that actually matters in *this* book is if you don't yet have a Twitter account or an online space—even an anonymous one—where you write down how you're experiencing and applying the ideas from this book.

On *this* path, you'll sign up for a Twitter account and follow every person you see mentioned in this book. You'll watch as they chat with people you don't know. You'll enjoy the insights and jokes and occasional cat pictures they broadcast to no one in particular.

Then, while you're reading this book, you may have a question, or want to clarify a term or technique. In this community, you can tweet that question to Lani and her interviewees as well. Do not wait for an introduction. In this community, your tweet will serve as a gentle tap on the shoulder. And I'll wager a cup of coffee you'll receive a response.

From there, you'll discover many more people walking along this path with you. You'll follow each other and send each other support and ideas. In that community, you'll make something of this book that its author and interviewees may not have anticipated. Their ideas will filter through your practice and produce unexpected successes and new insights. And that's where Lani's next book, or perhaps your first, will begin.

It's the kind of community that will celebrate your successes and sustain you through your failures in ways that other communities can't.

In the same way that your students will learn more math when they're communicating their ideas to you and to each other, you'll learn more from this book when you apply it and share your applications with other people. What makes this book special is that those other people can include its author and all the people she interviewed as well.

—Dan Meyer

ACKNOWLEDGMENTS

When we think about complex problems like those that arise in teaching, we often have many voices in our heads. These voices reflect different experiences and perspectives, and we may turn to them for the particular wisdom they have to offer. I spend a good deal of my professional life absorbing and understanding a wide range of voices: the teachers I work with and study, the students I teach, the scholars I read and argue with, as well as my own friends and family. The privilege of this work is that I have a chance to dwell on the voices I learn the most from, whether through analysis, conversations, reading, or writing.

This book has allowed me to bring a number of voices together to share my ideas about designing motivational math classrooms. My ideas come out of multiple ongoing conversations with a number of people. I am grateful to the teachers at Park City Math Institute (PCMI) who started this conversation with me, particularly Gail Burrill for extending the initial invitation to talk about helping students engage, and Cal Armstrong and Ashli Black for helping me identify a focus. I am indebted to the teachers of the Math Twitter Blogosphere (#MTBoS) for thoughtfully engaging with and sharing the blog post I wrote about the PCMI workshop, and to Heinemann editor, Katherine Bryant, for inviting me to submit a proposal for this book.

Because I am a researcher, I wanted to ground my ideas in studies about motivation and teaching. This phase of the project was supported by two outstanding Vanderbilt University graduate students: Julia Haltermann helped me collect and synthesize pertinent research literature, and Lara Heiberger worked with me to code and analyze the interviews with the featured teachers to connect research and practice. Once I had a draft, I was grateful for thoughtful readings from members of the Teacher Learning Laboratory at Vanderbilt: Grace Chen, Brette Garner, Lara Heiberger, Samantha Marshall, and Elizabeth Self. My dear colleague, Luis Leyva, gave the manuscript a close read to help me catch any gaps in relevant research. I further benefited from insightful comments from math teacher Michael Pershan and my teenage daughter Naomi Horn, as well as my Heinemann editor, Katherine Bryant.

Math teachers' voices are at the heart of this book. I am grateful to the featured teachers for sharing their thoughts about students, mathematics, and teaching. I am glad I have many pages devoted to show you their ideas, because without Peg Cagle, Rafranz Davis, Sadie Estrella, Chris Luzniak, Fawn Nguyen, and Elizabeth Statmore, this book would not be possible. Further contributions by #MTBoS folks, including Anna Blinstein, Tina Cardone, Andrew Gael, Heather Kohn, Justin Lanier, Dan Meyer, Paul Salomon, Anne Schwartz, Sara van der Werf, and Anna Weltman, fill out the illustrations of teachers' ingenuity in building inclusive and mathematically rich classrooms. I am further thankful to Dan Meyer for the gracious foreword that captures the collective wisdom of this incredible math teacher community. Undoubtedly, traces of countless other conversations with educators and scholars have found their way here: they have become second nature to my thinking and therefore beyond my consciousness for proper attribution and gratitude. As a blanket statement, let me be clear about how much I appreciate all the opportunities I have had to explore the things I care about with incredible people over the years. Finally, I thank my family, Adam, Naomi, Elinor, and Judah, for supporting me in pursuing the passion project that this book represents. I am grateful, as always, for their love, humor, and patience. Of course, any errors, oversights, or omissions remain my own.

INTRODUCTION

For the past several decades, leaders in mathematics education have emphasized that good instruction centers on student thinking. Despite a growing research base in support of this approach, teachers face numerous obstacles using classroom strategies that elicit, value, and build on students' mathematical ideas. These obstacles include traditions of schooling, students' prior experiences with mathematics, curricular constraints, and increases in skill-based standardized testing.

I have observed these challenges firsthand. Educators' efforts to implement what we have come to call "ambitious instruction" clearly push the status quo. *Ambitious instruction* is mathematics teaching that aims to engage *all* students in rich representations of content and authentic disciplinary practices, like justifying arguments, representing ideas, and modeling problems in the world.

In my research, I study how secondary mathematics teachers learn about instruction—ambitious and otherwise—in the contexts of their work. I have seen and documented the many challenges they face. I also have had the privilege of working with and studying the work of teachers who manage to overcome these challenges, engaging their students in problem solving and sense making. For instance, in my dissertation research, I taught in an urban high school mathematics department. The teachers helped me better understand how to implement ambitious instruction in ways I had never seen before, adapting Elizabeth Cohen and Rachel Lotan's Complex Instruction approach to mathematics classrooms

(Cohen and Lotan 2014). The Railside teachers, as they came to be known, worked together, identified and shared resources, and had a clearly articulated set of joint commitments in their teaching. When I talked to Railside students, I heard time and again about how much they enjoyed math class. It was a new and wonderful experience, and it left a deep impression on me. Changing the climate of math class had powerful effects on students' learning and persistence and their very identities as math learners.

When I moved to Seattle to work at the University of Washington, I collaborated with high school teachers to support ambitious instruction in their mathematics classrooms. We modeled our work on Railside and the teachers' use of Complex Instruction. We even took a group of Seattle teachers to California to visit Railside classrooms so they could see and interact with the teachers and students. By the end of the project, many teachers succeeded in shifting their instruction to center on students' thinking.

In this time, we saw how a positive social and emotional climate changed their students' experiences of math class, both increasing participation and raising overall achievement. I remember distinctly when one Seattle principal pulled me aside and told me that students kept telling him how much the math teachers "really cared" about them. This work was the basis of my previous book, *Strength in Numbers* (Horn 2012).

❯ The Challenge: Students Don't Want to Talk in Math Class

In the spring of 2014, I received a note from Gail Burrill, a colleague at Michigan State University who has run the Secondary Math Teachers Program at Park City Mathematics Institute (PCMI) for many years. In the program, math teachers come from around the country and spend three weeks of their summer doing cool mathematics problems and reflecting on teaching practice. Gail asked me if I could do a workshop with the teachers during the third week of PCMI. During the first two weeks, the teachers would be focusing on orchestrating classroom discussions with their students, learning particular practices for doing so. Could I talk about some implementation strategies to help them use the practices in their classrooms?

I agreed. In my preparation, I contacted two teacher facilitators for the program that summer, Cal Armstrong and Ashli Black. I asked them the same question: "What are the teachers saying about the classroom discussion practices over dinner?" They both told me the same thing. Outside of the workshop, many teachers expressed that this is all well and good, but it wouldn't work in a *real* classroom. Because, they felt, students do not like to talk about their mathematical thinking, the teachers could not imagine how these discussion practices would get off of the ground. This matches my experience in my own research: despite the best tools at teachers' disposal, students sat in stony silence or offered one- or two-word responses—and teachers provided scant intellectual press (Kazemi and Stipek 2001). Clearly, there is more to this practice than an invitation to an interesting problem by a well-meaning teacher.

As educators, our intention in asking students the questions "What do you think?" and "Why?" may be simply to build instruction around students' ideas. However, students often experience these questions quite differently. A central premise of this book is that eliciting student thinking involves *social risk*. In the public and evaluative classroom setting, students do a quick cost-benefit analysis: the cost of answering does not seem worth these potential risks. The discussion at my PCMI workshop, and discussion online after I blogged about it, helped me realize that math teachers everywhere were struggling with this part of ambitious instruction. That is, they liked the idea of orchestrating mathematical discussions, but they did not have adequate frameworks for decreasing the social risk and encouraging their students to share their ideas. These discussions led to this book.

> Finding Ideas That Work

In my studies of teacher learning, I have come to appreciate the need to combine any instructional framework ("here is what works") with rich and specific examples ("here is how it looks") to support teachers' understanding. Classroom teaching is complex and does not live in theoretical abstractions. To that end, I asked my online community, the #MTBoS (Math Twitter Blogosphere), to nominate secondary teachers who are really good at getting students to share mathematical ideas. To my great delight, I got a lot of names. In the end, I identified six teachers who:

- **Worked in a range of secondary grade levels and school settings.** The problems of (and therefore the solutions to) getting students to participate depend, in no small part, on who students are and what kinds of resources teachers have available.

- **Used different approaches to solving the problem of getting students to share their thinking.** I wanted to get away from simplistic discussions of "best practices." Instead of treating any one strategy as *the* way to get students to participate, I challenged myself to understand what different teachers' strategies have in common. (I'll say a little more about this later.)

- **Had a track record of writing or presenting on issues of mathematical discussions and class participation.** Explaining one's own teaching can be surprisingly hard, so I identified people who successfully communicate their instructional practice. They have written blogs, made videos, and given workshops—and if you find you have favorite teachers or practices, you can learn more about them through their writing.

Form and Function

Returning to the best practice idea, teachers often compare teaching approaches at the level of *form*—"I put my students in groups," "I use this textbook." The power of any approach or tool, however, depends on how they *function* in the classroom: What do students *do* in groups? How do you introduce the lessons in the textbook and use its various resources to support students' learning? In this book, for instance, you will be introduced to strategies called Counting Circles, Talking Points, Math Debates, and Visual Patterns. On the surface, these are distinct routines. Although the forms differ, they function in similar ways. On a deeper level, all of these strategies, as the featured teachers use them, support students' mathematical talk. In fact, thinking about the relation between the form and function of different teaching practices is one goal of this book.

Keep this form/function idea in mind as you are reading. This is not a *how to* reference, but rather a *why do* reference: I have organized the book by *why* the featured teachers' different practices foster students' motivation. In all likelihood, some strategies will better suit you, your students, and your school than others. By illustrating a range of strategies that can foster motivation, readers can identify methods that solve their particular teaching problems and fit their own personal practice and context, all while keeping their eye on the practice's purpose.

> About This Book

The first chapter of this book lays out a framework for a motivational math classroom. In it, I discuss five key factors that lead to a motivational classroom: belongingess, meaningfulness, competence, accountability, and autonomy. After I introduce you to the six featured teachers in Chapter 2, the following five chapters address each of these motivational factors in turn. In Chapter 8, I give you some ideas about how to build, change, and sustain your own practice as you work to implement and adapt this framework for your and your students' needs.

Along the way, I share examples not only from the six featured teachers, but from other colleagues in the #MTBoS. These additional pieces elaborate on main points or introduce some additional ideas or strategies.

Mathematics classrooms can be socially risky places for students. I hope you find this framework useful for thinking about designing your classroom in ways that lower social risk and motivate students to join in mathematical conversations.

MOTIVATED

1 | The Motivational Classroom

It is the second week of school. Students file into Ms. Gudinoff's eighth-grade classroom, some talking loudly with their friends as they settle in, a few sidling in quietly and sinking low in their seats. Ms. Gudinoff is at the front of the room, sorting papers and organizing her lesson materials. She feels a little nervous today. She is going to try something new: to engage students' mathematical thinking with a rich problem. She learned about leading mathematical discussions at last weekend's professional development workshop, part of her district's initiative to support deeper mathematical learning. After the bell rings, Ms. Gudinoff projects the following task on her SMART Board.

Directions: The larger figure below is a square. It has been partitioned into pieces. Each piece is identified with a letter.

Balanced Assessment: Middle Grades Assessment Package 1. Copyright © 1999. Reprinted by permission of Pearson Education, Inc., New York, NY.

"OK, we're going to try something new here," she announces. "I'd like you to get out a pencil and paper and spend five minutes quietly thinking about how you would find what fraction A is in this picture. Work by yourself first, then we can share our ideas." She colors in rectangle A on the SMART Board and writes, "What fraction of the square is A?" saying aloud, "OK, everybody got it?" She scans her class, sees a few nods, and hears a smattering of yeahs. After the students get out their materials, the next five minutes pass in relative silence, the sibilant undercurrent of whispering voices punctuated by scratching sounds of pencils on paper. As she watches her class at work, Ms. Gudinoff notices the following: a pair of girls, Mia and Riley, with their heads bent together over the problem; a handful of doodlers; one napper; several furrowed brows, with heads cradled in their hands; and many students stopping and starting as they make marks on their papers. She calls the class back together, saying, "OK, who wants to tell me how they started?" Looking around the room, the children appear frozen. She counts the seconds off in her head, remembering the importance of wait time. When she gets to fifteen, the silence starts to feel like a standoff: Who will break it first? It is Ms. Gudinoff. "Anyone have any ideas?" she tries again. Nothing. "Mia and Riley, I saw you discussing something. Can you share with the class?" The girls look mortified, as if she had asked them to do a chicken dance in front of their peers. Ms. Gudinoff sees a ripple of scowls and eye rolls pass across other students' faces, and Zachary mutters, "Not them again!"

Ms. Gudinoff had a lot going for her in this scenario. She had a rich problem with something discussable that had the potential to surface important ideas about fractions. She helped students focus on a reasonably small—but very doable—part to get them started, checking in to make sure they understood the task. She gave them a sensible amount of time to think quietly, giving some latitude to Mia and Riley, whom she knew gained confidence in discussing their ideas together. When her students seemed reluctant to share, she used the tried-and-true wait time strategy.

Nonetheless, when she called the class together to orchestrate a discussion, the students balked. Some students seemed to struggle to figure out what was being asked of them. Others were simply horrified of having their thinking on display in front of their peers. In any case, the mathematical discussion she was hoping to seed through this rich problem had no chance to take root. The ground of her classroom, it seems, was infertile for such activity.

▷ Social Risk

What does it take to create classroom climates that support and sustain mathematical conversations? To answer this question, we need to survey the landscape and identify what is making the environment inhospitable. We notice immediately that we are among a group of self-conscious adolescents. Indeed, students often avoid participating in mathematical discussions because publicly sharing their thinking is a *socially risky endeavor.* Social risk means *threats to one's status in a community.* Young people often come to school uncertain of their standing with their peers and teachers. At the same time, they are often highly preoccupied with their status. They tend toward activities that will be status enhancing—or at least, status preserving. They avoid activities that are status threatening, endangering their status in the eyes of their peers.

In planning her lesson, Ms. Gudinoff thought a lot about the mathematics of the task. She considered the different ideas students would have and how she would respond to them. She even took the time to give them a toehold into the problem, allowing five minutes of private think time before she asked them to share their ideas. What she did not account for was students' experience of being in her class: their sense of belonging, what this activity meant to them in their lives, their concerns about looking smart or dumb in front of their peers. These are the central issues of social risk.

Typical math lessons can proceed without accounting for social risk because they rely primarily on *known-answer* questions. Known-answer questions are less risky because students have models or prior examples to draw on when they respond. If a class has spent a week talking about linear equations, many students do not find risk in answering:

$$\textit{What is the slope in } y = 4x - 2?$$

This known-answer question only requires students to remember the slope-intercept form of $y = mx + b$ and successfully match the slope (m) to the 4. There might even be a cue in a student's homework or notes that lets the student answer without understanding.

However, the social risk increases when a teacher asks:

$$\textit{What do you think will happen to the graph if I change}$$
$$\textit{the slope to } -4\textit{? Explain your reasoning.}$$

This second question requires students to *predict, make connections* between equations and graphs, and *justify their reasoning.* Students cannot easily draw cues without understanding. They must grasp underlying ideas about positive and negative slopes. Although these practices are an important part of mathematical thinking, they are difficult to elicit in mathematics classrooms because of the social risk involved.

Social risk also depends on students' relationships to their peers. In the opening vignette, Mia and Riley may have had some confidence in their approach, but Zachary's muttering shows some of their peers' resentment for their level of investment. Even when students have ideas, they may be reluctant to share them because of the risk posed to their social status.

Mathematics Classrooms as Socially Risky Places

Although social risk is felt in many classrooms, mathematics classrooms are particularly burdened with social risk. Mathematics, as a school subject, is culturally anointed as the ultimate measure of smartness. The logic goes: If you are good at math, you are truly smart. If you are not good at math, you are not truly smart. Many of us, as mathematics educators, have encountered competent adults who confess their insecurity over not being "good at math." Because of the linking of mathematics and "true" smartness, when students share their thinking in the public space of the classroom, they often perceive risks to their academic status that go beyond the immediate content, extending instead to their overall intelligence.

Adolescence as a Socially Risky Time

Adolescents have two things going on that heighten the risk of sharing their thinking. First, they have years of history with math class as an evaluative environment that hampers them from sharing their ideas—especially when they are only partially formed—out of fear of looking foolish or dumb in front of their peers. Exacerbating this, adolescent students are increasingly aware of and dependent on their peers' approval, especially compared with their time in the primary grades. This leads to particular challenges for secondary teachers who want to elicit students' ideas. When students compare participation's risks (e.g., losing face in front of their peers) to its perceived benefits (e.g., pleasing a teacher), they often calculate that it is not worth doing.

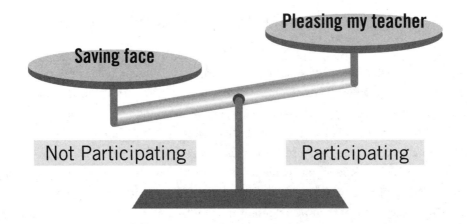

This poses a conundrum for mathematics teachers who want to teach ambitiously. Meaningful mathematical learning, which is the goal of ambitious instruction, involves exploration, false starts, and confusion on the way to deeper understanding. How are teachers to persuade students to engage in such socially risky activities at a time in their development where they are least likely to want to participate in them?

> Designing Motivating Instruction

The answer offered here lies in instructional design. By *design*, I am not referring to a prescribed set of routines, activities, or seating arrangements. Instead, I offer a framework for thinking through teaching choices in ways that attend to motivational issues and support students' participation. Motivation, in this context, goes beyond the everyday sense of the word, which usually means getting students excited or interested in mathematics by couching problems in contexts that appeal to their adolescent sensibilities like pop culture, sports, fashion, or music. Instead, the motivational framework I describe attends to the social and emotional conditions that students need to participate effectively in mathematical activities.

Designing to motivate is a familiar practice to many people. For instance, we may all "know" that it is healthier to satisfy a sweet tooth with an apple than with ice cream, but faced with both foods as a snack option, we do not always make the healthiest choice. (This may or may not be an autobiographical example.) Knowing our own weaknesses, we can design our environments to make fruit more readily available than sweets. My favorite example of motivationally oriented design comes from Odenplan subway station in Stockholm, Sweden. To encourage more people to take the stairs instead of the escalator at the subway passage, a group called FunTheory.com covered the stairs with piano keys. (If you have seen the movie *Big*, you can picture the giant piano that resulted. Or just search for "subway piano stairs" on YouTube.) With the new design, 66 percent more people took the stairs than the escalator, simply because it was motivating to have the chance to play instead of a drag to take the stairs. Putting up signs about the health benefits of stairs fails to motivate a typical commuter, just as seeing the nutrition label on an ice cream container does not always motivate me to eat an apple. This is the goal of motivationally oriented design: helping people to engage in beneficial behaviors not by merely informing them of their value but also by making them easy and desirable.

For teachers to motivate social risk taking, they must look at the classroom environment and find ways to change the risk-taking calculus. By putting piano keys on the stairs, the designers shifted *taking the stairs* from an objectively better but actually less appealing choice to the amusing and desirable choice. The stairs were no longer the *harder* option but instead became the *fun* option. This kind of design thinking changes people's cost-benefit calculus: the cost of taking the stairs is far outweighed by the benefit of playing the piano while walking on them.

In a similar way, we, as teachers, need to design instruction and classroom spaces that lower the risks and raise the benefits of participation. To lower the risks, for instance, we need to work against students' assumptions about mathematical smartness and make socially safe spaces for students to be wrong without losing face in front of their peers. To increase the benefits, we need to design instruction where students feel *invited*—even compelled!—to share their thinking. In fact, in truly motivational classrooms, *not* taking risks—withholding thinking—becomes a less attractive option for students and their learning, just as the escalator became a less attractive option than the piano stairs.

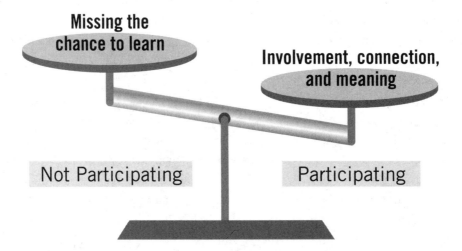

To develop this motivational framework, I draw on the work of psychologists who study the social and relational aspects of motivation, translating these theoretical ideas into principles for instructional design. The work of psychologist Julianne Turner and her colleagues (2014) provides a great starting point. They spent three years collaborating with middle school teachers around central ideas about motivation to support deeper learning and shift students' social risk calculus. Their work with teachers focused on applying four motivational constructs to instructional design: belongingness, meaningfulness, competence, and autonomy. Over many decades of research, social psychology has linked these constructs to motivation. Because teachers work in classrooms and need ways to engineer student behavior, I add a fifth construct—accountability—that provides the feedback mechanisms that help shape students' participation. In the chapters ahead, I illustrate each of these five constructs with examples from the featured teachers' classrooms. Because these constructs need to work together in any teacher's practice, I offer an overview of the framework here to help readers envision how they might work in concert to create mathematics classrooms that reflect motivational instructional design.

Features of a Motivational Classroom

A motivational classroom attends to the following five features:

- students' sense of *belongingness*
- the *meaningfulness* of learning
- students' *competence*
- structures for *accountability*
- students' *autonomy.*

Teachers can foster all of these through deliberate instructional design as they tinker to motivate their students.

Belongingness refers to people's innate need to establish close relationships with others. In the opening vignette, the students who slinked down into their desks, doing everything physically possible to make themselves disappear, communicated with their body language that they did not feel like they belong. In contrast, when students experience frequent, pleasant interactions with others or feel that those around them are concerned for their well-being, they feel like they belong. Although Ms. Gudinoff's classroom climate would benefit from numerous adjustments, something as simple as a warm greeting as students enter the door might go a long way toward helping the reluctant ones trust that they belong there. This, in turn, can pay dividends in participation. Research has linked students' sense of relatedness and belonging to social and academic engagement (Stipek et al. 1998; Furrer and Skinner 2003). In general, teachers can foster a sense of belongingness by encouraging and modeling an environment of mutual respect. In our vignette, this might include addressing Zachary and other students' disdain for Mia and Riley's enthusiasm.

Meaningfulness involves developing an interest in or appreciation for academic content. Every math teacher gets asked the same question at one point or another: When are we ever going to use this? Instead of viewing this question as students' resistance or reluctance to learn, we should understand that they are often searching for meaningfulness. When students experience their learning as connected to their own lives or questions, it raises engagement and achievement (Wigfield and Eccles 2007). Teachers can cultivate meaningful learning by building on students' prior knowledge and experiences, providing access to complex ideas and extended exploration. Perhaps Ms. Gudinoff could have related the fractions question to children's persistent concerns about sharing. Teachers can also model meaningfulness by emphasizing their own interest in and the value they place on what they are teaching.

Competence describes the need to be successful in meeting goals and interacting with the environment (Wigfield and Eccles 2007). By the time students arrive in our classrooms, they have often had many experiences feeling *in*competent in mathematics. This comes from countless sources: they have not been able to succeed on the "mad minute" fact tests, a state assessment has labeled them as "basic" in their mathematical proficiency, or family members or other teachers have let them know that "some people are just not math people." Because school math commonly values two primary forms of mathematical competence—quickness and accuracy—students have seldom had a chance to recognize their own mathematical strengths. Teachers can increase students' sense of competence by providing appropriately challenging tasks, giving formative feedback, and helping students recognize their own mathematical strengths. Teachers can also increase students' sense of competence by normalizing mistakes as opportunities to grow and learn. This fosters effort and persistence.

Accountability refers to the structures and routines that oblige students to report, explain, or justify their activities. Often reduced simply to *assessment*, accountability goes beyond how we grade to encompass the routines and norms that enjoin students to participate in particular ways in classroom life. When students feel a sense of investment in and accountability to their classmates, for example, this changes the risk-benefit calculus, leveraging positive peer pressure to increase participation. Likewise, if students have some say in their activities or understand the relationship between those activities and their personal goals, they will have a greater sense of commitment to seeing them through (Fielding 2001). Research has shown that accountability systems that provide ongoing feedback for learning help close achievement disparities and support students in developing self-regulation of their own learning (Stiggins and Chappuis 2005).

Autonomy is the need to behave according to one's interests and values. The opposite of autonomy is dependence; most math teachers have encountered students who ask for help at every step of a problem, because they have not yet developed their own resources for making sense of their work and seeing it through. Autonomy can be seen in the classroom when students pursue their own curiosities, work to organize their schoolwork, and contribute to the classroom community. Research has linked autonomy to numerous positive outcomes, including staying in school, deeper conceptual learning, seeking intellectual challenge, and enjoying academic work (Turner et al. 2014). Teachers can inculcate student autonomy by linking instruction to students' strengths and interests, giving meaningful reasons for learning different content, allowing students the time they need to learn, and valuing different ways of thinking about ideas.

Connecting the Motivational Features

There are many connections across these five motivational features.

For example, *belongingness* and *meaningfulness* are mutually reinforcing, because *belongingness* implies that students' own interests and curiosity have found a place in the classroom. This provides fodder for an alert teacher to build meaningful mathematical activities. Likewise, *accountability* and *autonomy* are connected. If classrooms are designed in ways that press students to feel *accountable* to one another's learning, this will foster *autonomy*, as students develop ways to function using their own resources and not solely rely on teachers, textbooks, or the "smarter" students. *Competence* contributes to a sense of mathematical legitimacy and thereby increases students' sense of belongingness. These are just a few examples. Others will be explored in the pages ahead.

2 | Meet the Teachers

Throughout this book, I illustrate the motivational classroom framework using the instructional practices of six teachers. To give you a sense of who these teachers are, in this chapter, I introduce you to them, their settings, and their guiding philosophies.

Oftentimes, conversations about good teaching presume that the magic comes entirely in the *how*—how teachers set up their classrooms, develop routines, organize their lessons. Our focus on how too often overlooks the urgent question of *why:* why they arrange their desks in rows, review homework in class, or make sure to start the day with a class discussion. Our inattention to why leads educators to take sweeping positions: putting students in rows is *always* a bad idea; reviewing homework *never* works; class discussions only work with *some* kids. Although these positions may reflect some teachers' experiences, they are far too expansive about what does and does not work and do not dig into why these assertions are being made. Each school, each teacher, and each classroom community has different strengths and limitations. Not all instructional practices are equally feasible in every setting. This may sound at first like a completely undecided stance—as if everything is all equally good. But that is not my intent. Instead, by digging deeper into the shared purposes across a range of practices in different settings, we can have more robust ideas about how and why certain approaches achieve motivational goals in different classroom settings.

In this spirit, instead of foregrounding how the featured teachers organized their classrooms, I focus on why their designs motivated students to participate. I hope that you can take up and purposefully adapt their ideas to create your own motivational math classrooms. I provide general descriptions of the featured teachers' practices here, with additional information available in the appendix so you can learn more about any approaches you are interested in pursuing in greater depth.

Without further ado, let us meet the teachers.

Teacher	Grades Taught	School Type	School Size	Student Demographics	Signature Teaching Practices
Peg Cagle	Middle school	Urban school with gifted magnet program	1,700	50% Latino 20% white 20% Asian 10% emergent bilinguals 60% free or reduced-price lunch	Playful Problems
Rafranz Davis	High school	Small city comprehensive	1,600	50% Latino 30% white 10% African American 60% free or reduced-price lunch	Math Through Exploration and Making
Sadie Estrella	High school	K–12 rural community	350	80% Native Hawaiian 80% free or reduced-price lunch	Counting Circles
Chris Luzniak	High school	Urban academic theme school	500	70% Black 20% Latino 80% free or reduced-price lunch	Math Debates with Claims and Warrants
Fawn Nguyen	K–8 school	Suburban comprehensive school	600	60% Latino 30% White 20% emergent bilinguals 40% free or reduced-price lunch	Visual Patterns and Playful Problems
Elizabeth Statmore	High school	Urban gifted magnet	2,500	60% Asian 15% white 10% Latino 50% free or reduced-price lunch	Talking Points

A summary of the teachers, their most recent school at the time of my interviews, and their signature teaching practices. Student demographics are rounded for simplicity and only reported if a category was at or above 10 percent of the population. I use "Black" to describe the students at Chris Luzniak's school to reflect the diversity of Caribbean and African-immigrant students who identified as Black but not necessarily African American.

As you read these teachers' stories about how their practices evolved, you may note some similarities. They are all engaged in ongoing professional learning, always striving to get better at what they do. They enjoy the puzzles of teaching and take particular satisfaction in helping students connect to mathematics in new and deeper ways. Undoubtedly, they all strive toward positive classroom climates that are inclusive and support rich mathematical learning. They also share an abiding curiosity about students' thinking.

At the same time, as I learned about their instructional approaches, it is clear that there is not a single set of prescriptions for "best practice" in the usual sense of that idea. They have different entry points for engaging their students and employ a range of strategies that reflect their own strengths as thinkers as well as the needs and assets of the communities they serve.

❯ Peg Cagle

At the time of our interview, Peg Cagle had taught middle school in Los Angeles Unified School District for seventeen years. When Peg was in elementary school, she fell in love with math through the post-Sputnik New Math curriculum. Although it was later subject to much derision, the New Math problems captured young Peg, who loved set theory and doing non–base ten arithmetic. Later, Peg became a licensed architect, steeped in practical applications of mathematics. She continues to be an avid mathematical learner and enjoys the beauty of pure math, conveying a deep enthusiasm for both to her students.

Peg became enthralled with teaching as an adjunct faculty in an architecture school where she taught about human behavior and design. As Peg explained to me, architecture must attend to form *and* function: buildings are not just big sculptures—they're actually places used and occupied by people. As she developed her teaching practice, she applied her architectural training: it was another place replete with the problems of designing spaces for people to do things—in this case, learning. She decided to pursue secondary teaching full time.

When I talk to Peg about her classroom, I can see her design thinking at every turn. Teaching in an urban public school certainly comes with its fair share of design challenges. As just one of many examples, one year she was assigned an eighth-grade sheltered class for emergent bilingual students with thirty students speaking seven different languages. Because some of the students had not had any formal schooling, the students' ages ranged from thirteen to sixteen. Peg described the class as "running four preps in one room," using manipulatives to teach basic calculations without words to some students, while finding grade-appropriate, minimally language dependent problems for others. Most of the time,

Peg's classroom centers on Playful Problems, which provide touchstone experiences she can refer back to over time and give her a context for students' sense making. As a result, she is a collector of many mathematical toys and materials. My own children call Peg their mathematical fairy godmother. She has a mischievous twinkle in her eye as she poses interesting questions and helps students learn to mathematize the world.

Playful Problems

Peg designs her classroom to support problem-based mathematics learning. She sets up intriguing situations in the form of Playful Problems. These are rich mathematical contexts that point to important ideas. They can vary in specificity and structure, but they all allow students to investigate while she asks them questions to help them dig out the mathematics.

When Peg talks about Playful Problems, she explains how she wants her students to "muck about" with the mathematics, exploring what she presents and raising their own questions. These lessons anchor a set of ideas for her students, giving the class a shared reference point through a unit of study and beyond.

As one example, she had her geometry students roll plastic cups on their tables and describe the shape they traced as they rolled around. After making conjectures about the shape, they could generate other questions. What was its area? How could you find it? How would you know? Through this exploration, they had to justify their ideas and try to convince their classmates.

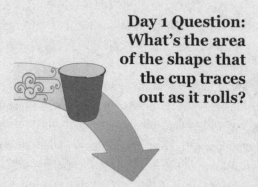

Day 1 Question: What's the area of the shape that the cup traces out as it rolls?

This particular lesson became a touchstone for a months-long exploration of area, circumference, inductive reasoning, and parallel and perpendicular lines, as well as highlighting the need for clear definitions. Sometimes, Peg does more to structure the inquiry, but the climate of exploration and conjecturing is still there. Peg uses a structured Playful Problem to model exponential growth. She has her students start with a piece of art tissue paper and tells them to fold it in half repeatedly and identify how many rectangular layers the paper has with each fold. They track the data in a chart, tracking the number of folds and number of rectangles, to explore the pattern. This becomes the basis for a generalization about exponential growth: How many layers would I have if I could fold the paper 100 times? 1,000? *N* times?

> Rafranz Davis

Rafranz Davis taught middle school and high school for eight years in a small Texas city. Rafranz's story of becoming an educator has an air of inevitability. Her mother, Beverly Davis, worked as a teacher's aide in her Texas hometown. As an African American woman working with African American students, Rafranz's mother built deep relationships that Rafranz described as "a miracle to watch." Mrs. Davis had a strong commitment to her community, and, to this end, she would bring a young (and often reluctant) Rafranz with her to church to tutor high school seniors who needed to pass the math section of a graduation exam. Despite her hesitation, it was there Rafranz first felt the exhilaration of helping somebody understand an idea that they had previously struggled with. Later, in college, she helped keep a distraught roommate from failing a math course by holding a last-minute, crash-course study session.

Even though the deep satisfaction of teaching bubbled up again, she squelched it awhile longer, taking a job in industry. "One day, I was driving to work and I stopped and said, 'You need to turn around and go back to school [to become a teacher].' And I did." Her choice of math also seems equally destined: Rafranz describes math as her "happy place." As a child, she would look for the hardest problems in her math books and work on them for fun.

Following her mother's example, Rafranz develops deep relationships with her students. She makes a point of knowing their interests and strengths outside of school. She has a widely read blog as well as a book (Davis 2015a, 2015b), and much of her writing focuses on what it means to truly engage students, especially reluctant learners. A strong proponent of educational technology and MakerSpaces, she is not blinded by the high-flying promises of these tools: she advocates for meaningful learning, calling out the techno-euphoria that oversells shiny new tools for the same old uses. As she reflected in a blog post, "Kids . . . are not 'tricked' by the technology that we throw at them to mask activities with no purpose" (Davis 2013).

Listening to Rafranz talk and reading her words, one quickly ascertains that she is a keen observer of students. As one example, she described what she calls "the seat assessment," a strategy of watching where her students sit when they come to her class on the first day of school. "The ones who thought they would be terrible, who had really big issues with math, often sat at the back, and everyone else sat toward the front, and the ones who were kind of halfway sat in the middle" (Davis 2014a). Without realizing it, her students gave her important information about their mathematical confidence. She attributes her care in observing students to her mother. As another example of how much she learns by watching her students, she put a MakerShelf in her classroom. A perpetual MakerSpace, it was a place for students to create and explore. Rafranz observed what students made to get a better sense of who they were as learners and then displayed some of their creations in her room. Rafranz's deep mathematical knowledge, empathy for students, and focus on meaningful engagement resonate in her writing and speaking. (One of the great pleasures of following Rafranz's social media accounts involves watching her nurture the creativity of her nephew, Braeden. He is an incredible artist, and his auntie Rafranz shares his projects, as well as her advocacy to help his teachers appreciate his gifts. See Davis 2014b for one example.)

> Sadie Estrella

At the time of our interview, Sadie Estrella was in her eleventh year as an educator. Growing up in Hawai'i, Sadie had a fascination with sharks. She originally went to university to study biology and research the fierce and wild creatures. Once in college in California, she realized that lab work did not excite her, but she loved her mathematics courses. "I'm a math nerd," she told me. "I love studying math with people. I love talking about math with people." Sadie got a degree in mathematics with a focus on secondary education. She also mastered sign language, with the intention of teaching deaf students. Although she had an opportunity to stay on the mainland and teach at a deaf school, she missed her friends and family in Hawai'i and returned there to start her career.

For her first eight years, Sadie was the sole high school math teacher in a small, rural PreK–12 school in Maui. She worked primarily with native Hawai'ian students, the majority of whom lived in poverty. Her school had high dropout rates, particularly in the high school grades. When Sadie arrived there, she worked hard to build the curriculum and persuade her students to trust her. Sadie is not native Hawai'ian and does not speak Ōlelo Hawai'i, the indigenous language, but she often slips into Hawai'ian pidgin, a mix of English and Ōlelo Hawai'i, in the middle of a story. A light-skinned Latina, Sadie's fluency in this dialect aided her connection with her students. "When I open my mouth, then they're like, 'Oh no, she's not white. She's born and raised here.'" In addition to her love of math, Sadie has an unending curiosity about people. Through shared cultural connections and from her genuine interest in them, her students learned to trust her.

Sadie faced one major challenge in her teaching: many of her high school students had not yet developed strong computational fluency. Determined to meet them where they were while progressing in the high school curriculum, Sadie adapted Jessica Shumway's Counting Circles for her classroom (Shumway 2011). Although Shumway's routines are designed for elementary children, Sadie increased the mathematical demands for her older students by recording their answers on number lines, a central representation in algebra.

Sadie's way of meeting this challenge reflects her philosophy of caring for her students while giving them the skills to be successful. Instead of engaging in the "blame game," pointing the finger at prior teachers for her students' math knowledge (most of whom, it should be noted, worked in her same small school), Counting Circles gave Sadie a strategy for addressing the students' challenges. She knew that improving their arithmetic and number sense would bring up their confidence while providing a stronger base for high school mathematics topics. It also gave a basis for talking about their thinking.

It took Sadie a few years of trial and error to develop these teaching strategies. She kept at it because she believed in her kids. "When we treat students like human beings and we honor who they are," she told me, "they will honor you back and they will want to be part of this community. That's how I learned about creating a community in my classroom, from these kids."

ounting Circles

Sadie uses a Counting Circles routine for about ten minutes at the start of class. To begin, you need a *starting number* and a *counting number*.

For example, you can start at 17 and count by –3.
Sadie sets the ground rules:

- No need to rush. Take your time.
- Do not comment on other people's answers.
- If you make a mistake, it is OK.
- If you notice somebody's mistake, ask a question. Do not correct.

Sadie has a volunteer go first. Then students continue counterclockwise to say the next count. She writes down each number as they say it, without comment about whether it is correct.

After going around the circle once, she finds a place to stop. She then asks the group to predict what somebody further down the circle is going to say. She asks students to signal that they have a prediction by raising their thumbs, a small signal that lets her know they have an answer without distracting other students. She waits for all thumbs to come up, and then she starts the *number talk* portion of the routine. Here, she gathers about three different strategies students used to predict what the number would be.

"Counting is amazing," Sadie tells me. "Counting will let you know kids' strengths and weaknesses. You will see kids counting on their fingers, counting by tens, counting in the air. That's when they started sharing and discussing."

> Chris Luzniak

Chris Luzniak studied theatre and mathematics at a small liberal arts college in his native Ohio. Through his undergraduate years, he grew more interested in mathematics, entering a doctoral program after graduation. When he completed his master's degree, he realized that he enjoyed teaching undergraduate calculus more than he liked doing research, so he decided to teach full time. He attended a one-year credential program in New York City, moving into a teaching position at a small, theme-based high school in New York City's public schools. Students enrolled from the city's five boroughs, many enduring long daily train commutes to and from the Brooklyn school. The vast majority of students qualified for free or reduced-priced lunch and faced the adversity that comes with poverty, and they were academically ambitious, as was reflected in the school's consistently high attendance and college matriculation rates, both of which exceeded 90 percent.

With his background in undergraduate teaching, Chris primarily taught math to the school's seniors, although in his eight years there, he ended up teaching "a little bit of everything." Drawing on his theatre experience, Chris also worked as the school's debate coach. His math department consisted of around half a dozen like-minded colleagues (staffing fluctuated over the years), many of whom participated in the Math for America professional development program, which emphasizes ambitious teaching in urban classrooms. For most of Chris' tenure, the math department had a climate of support, sharing, and mutual respect. Only in the last two years did that culture shift, as accountability pressures mounted along with increased scrutiny from test-based teacher evaluations, leading to a greater emphasis on test preparation.

Chris took an interest in having students discuss their thinking about two years into teaching. He attended a professional development workshop that helped him see that talking about math was a separate—and equally important—skill than writing about math. Because of his work as the debate coach, he got the idea to incorporate debate into math class. When he tried it out, he spent a long time planning the ten-minute debates, resulting in about five tries that first year. Over time, he developed routines for preparing and doing debates in his classroom, making them a regular part of his instruction. A fortuitous connection with a nonprofit organization seeking to incorporate debate across the curriculum provided him with even more structures and tools for using debates with his students.

"Almost anything is debatable if you ask it in the right way," Chris told me. Some of his questions are about process: What is the best way to start this problem? More mathematically, students might get a card with "1.78778777877778 . . ." and have to debate whether or not it is rational. "Teenagers love to share their opinions, so they're eager to do the problems for me when it's more opinion, even though they're doing the math."

lath Debates

Chris first introduces his classes to debates using a nonmathematical topic, like, "The best movie ever is _____" or "The most powerful superhero is _____." The debate structure requires that students make an *argument*, which consists of a *claim* and a *warrant*. He provides students with a sentence frame for making their argument, posting signs that say:

My CLAIM is _____,

and my WARRANT is _____.

Verbally, he instructs the debate to proceed with the following rules:

1. When you are called on, you must stand.

2. You must use the words, "My claim is . . ." and "my warrant is . . ."

3. If you are not speaking, your shoulders and knees must turn toward the speaker.

4. Our eyes should be on the speaker (who should be standing).

5. Only the person standing is speaking. The rest of us are listening.

6. When you respond, summarize what the person before you said.

During the first debates, he asks students to volunteer to make an argument. He makes sure they follow all the rules he set up, modeling the debate structure for other students. Depending on the topic, he has between three and five people share their arguments. Once students grow familiar with the debate structure, he introduces mathematical topics for them to argue.

> Fawn Nguyen

Fawn Nguyen's love of math goes all the way back to high school, when she would seek out problems to do. Many educators talk about voracious readers: Fawn, it seems, was a voracious problem solver. She studied science in college in Oregon and spent the first part of her teaching career as a science teacher. One summer, she took a problem-solving class with former National Council of Teachers of Mathematics President Michael Shaughnessy, which rekindled her love for mathematics. "I found myself really struggling; I loved it. I loved it because I don't have all the answers! I worked on this for two days, and I can't eat dinner because I'm stuck on this. I loved solving problems!"

When family circumstances brought her to California, she decided to seize the opportunity to teach her great love: mathematics. At the time I interviewed her, she had taught sixth- and eighth-grade math for eleven years at the same K–8 suburban school. On the first day of her first math class, she brought one of her favorite problems (Fawn's students would tell you every problem is her favorite problem), *The Pudding Problem*, to her middle school students (NCTM n.d.). She had some success engaging her students, but she realized that she needed more instructional strategies to help all of her students see how amazing rich problems could be. There were numerous teaching puzzles she had to sort out, including how hard it was to tell what students actually understood. She knew she wanted to teach mathematics using her favorite problems, but she needed more teaching tools at her disposal. Through a combination of her own tinkering and good professional development, she began to focus on classroom discussions. Undoubtedly, though, the problems themselves are at the core of her math classroom. "If you don't have the right task," she told me, "there's no rich discussions to begin with."

Problems are the center of her teaching, and she especially likes playful problems with her middle school students. In one example, *The Barbie Bungee*, students have to make predictions by building a linear function. Here is how she sets up the problem:

OBJECTIVE: Create a bungee line for Barbie to allow her the most thrilling, yet SAFE, fall from a height of three meters.

I randomly assigned students to groups of three. Each group got their own Barbie and seven new same-size rubber bands. My instructions:

1. Measure Barbie's height. Record this as rubber band length of 0.

2. Connect two rubber bands with a slipknot.

3. Wrap one of the two rubber bands tightly around Barbie's ankles.

4. Drop Barbie, holding the rubber band level with the meter stick.

5. Record Barbie's fall using the lowest point her head reaches in centimeters. This number is your rubber band length of 1. (The rubber band around her ankle is not counted in the length of the line.)

6. Add another rubber band, drop Barbie, and record. Do this for a total of six rubber band lengths.

7. Use the data to graph rubber band lengths versus distance of fall. Use the graph to predict how many rubber bands Barbie would need for the maximum ride without cracking her head open.

Visual Patterns

Fawn starts her classes off with a visual pattern routine twice a week. When students arrive, they see a pattern projected on the screen. These range from simple to complex geometric figures, varying in dimension and color. Once the bell rings for class to begin, Fawn instructs students to look at the pattern quietly for two to five minutes, allowing more time for complex patterns. After the allotted time passes, she has students turn to a partner to discuss what they noticed. Then, she calls on three students at random to explain how they saw the pattern and if they have an equation for it. After hearing those responses, she asks the rest of the students if they had a different way of looking at the pattern. During the discussion, Fawn asks questions like, "Could you draw the next step in the pattern?" and "What would step 27 look like? How do you know?" This routine helps students develop mathematical generalizations and practice justification. Because it gets repeated over time, Fawn's students start to recognize common strategies. Nothing delights her more when they refer back to previously used strategies, saying things like, "I did what Joey did the other day." This lets her know her students are listening and learning over time, a strong signal that they understand the mathematical meaning of their activity.

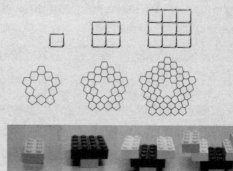

After the students make their predictions from the data, they then test them ou videos Fawn has posted of this moment, the students are rapt with attention, full o ticipation as their teacher climbs on a ladder to test their claims, cheering excitedly when Barbie makes her fall without banging her head.

Fawn finds math problems everywhere and helps her students learn to do the same. She uses a number of discourse structures to help students think about these problems. (See some of the discussions from her students at http://www.mathtalks.net/.) She has two routines that she uses daily in her class: Visual Patterns and Mental Math. She has focused a lot on her questioning, and she prompts students to listen and respond to each other's ideas. She also draws on routines like Notice and Wonder (Ray 2013) or the 5 Practices (Stein and Smith 2011). But beyond that, Fawn values what she calls The Five *Fs*—(1) *fast:* giving students a lot of feedback quickly; (2) *fair:* giving each child what they need; (3) *friendly:* which is not the same as being a friend; (4) *firm:* not being strict but having structures and then following through; and (5) *funny:* being playful and silly. "Building relationships trumps everything," she said during a talk. "It makes teaching not about surviving but thriving."

Mental Math Talks

Mental Math Talks are five- to fifteen-minute discussions whose primary goal is computational fluency, defined as "having efficient and accurate methods for computing" (National Council of Teachers of Mathematics 2000). Students show this when they can flexibly choose methods, as well as explain and understand them, all while producing accurate answers.

Fawn poses Mental Math tasks twice a week at the start of class. These can be straightforward computations ("What is 433 + 129?") or slightly trickier ("What is 35% of 90?"). The key is that students figure out the answer mentally, quietly signaling the teacher when they have completed the computation. Several students share their answers. These answers are treated like conjectures, proposals for an answer. In this spirit, several others share *how* they arrived at their answers. The teacher records and facilitates this process. Finally, the class, as a whole, agrees on the answer for the problem, discussing which models make the most sense to students and what they found convincing. (Fawn writes about her Mental Math Talks in her Math Talks blog [Nguyen n.d.].)

⫸ Elizabeth Statmore

Elizabeth Statmore had two careers prior to becoming a mathematics teacher. First, she was a Dante scholar, studying comparative literature at Stanford. Like many young people around the Silicon Valley during that era, she got drawn into the excitement of the high-tech industry. That brought her to her second career in software marketing. She worked in the industry for over two decades. During an economic downturn, she took a sabbatical to work on a writing project and soon realized that she wanted to change paths yet again. Her time in Silicon Valley gave her a deep appreciation for the gatekeeping role of calculus and the way it pushed many people out. "I saw how so many smart, interesting people had already kind of opted themselves out of the leadership pipeline long before they could make informed decisions about pathways and opportunities," she told me. "I would like to help more people of good character get through the calculus pipeline."

Led by this vision for her work, Elizabeth was in her sixth year as a high school math teacher at the time of our interview. Having a strong humanities background herself, she saw how many capable students struggled in mathematics for nonacademic reasons. "Social and emotional learning stands to have the biggest payoff in mathematics education," she told me. During our conversation, she pointed out that mathematics education, as a field, has not done enough in this arena. I concurred, noting that much of the research on inviting students into classroom discussions has focused on elementary classrooms. "With older kids," she said, "their defense mechanisms are just so much more activated."

In addition to her academic and marketing background, Elizabeth has studied mindfulness meditation, a practice that helps people to be fully present in what they are doing without feeling reactive or otherwise overwhelmed. She draws on these ideas as a framework for supporting her students' math learning. As she explained to me, "What works about meditation practice was this notion of having a structure and—no matter what—you stay with the structure for the full period of time. Having the anchor of the practice gives you a safe structure for noticing what is going on." Connecting this insight to her classroom teaching, Elizabeth looked for some kind of discourse structure to ease her students' trepidation around talking in mathematics class. Her solution was to adapt psychologist Neil Mercer's Talking Points (Mercer and Hodgkinson 2008) to the secondary mathematics classroom, a topic on which she has written and presented extensively. In the spirit of mindfulness, Talking Points supports students' exploratory talk, helping them to observe their own thinking processes in a nonjudgmental way.

Talking Points

Usually, math classrooms focus on students giving correct answers more than exploring ideas, so Elizabeth uses Talking Points to help students engage in and listen to each other's rough draft talk. Students get into groups of three and are given a set amount of time to respond, one by one, to a series of statements, saying whether they agree, disagree, or are unsure, along with a reason for their position. Students go around the circle twice, with the option to change their mind the second time through.

The statements vary depend on Elizabeth's goals. Sometimes they are statements about learning ("Just because you have heard something doesn't mean you understand it right away"), but more often, they are about the mathematics her classes are studying ("Every linear function has a y-intercept"). By exploring their own ideas in a small-group setting that is also designed to support listening to others, students have a chance to articulate their thinking and make deeper connections.

> What Do We Take Away from These Stories?

I am fascinated by the persistence of talk about best practices in teaching, as if these could be captured at the level of what teachers do. Clearly, the featured teachers approach their instruction differently: their classrooms and their instructional routines all look different. Yet they all succeed in getting their diverse students to share their mathematical ideas.

As I said earlier, I have long suspected that best practices do not live in the descriptions of *how* teachers teach but rather in *why* they make the choices they do. As different as they are on some level, the featured teachers share an enthusiasm for their subject, a deep respect for and curiosity about their students, and a habit of reflecting on their practice as they strive to make it better. What they do works in their various settings because of this similar stance rather than because of similarities in their instructional organization.

I also suspect that *who* we are as teachers shapes what we can do to reach the students we teach. For instance, some of my students expressed that it mattered that I was a female precalculus teacher, because I served as a role model by teaching upper-level math courses. Less obviously, some of my Muslim students connected with me around being a religious minority (I am Jewish), making jokes about our holidays that seldom fell in line with the school calendar and the challenges of our different dietary traditions. During my interviews with the featured teachers, they differently described the salience of their racial, ethnic, or linguistic backgrounds. For some teachers, it informed their relationships with students in very clear ways. For others, it did not. There are a couple of possible reasons for this. As I explained earlier, much of what teachers do remains outside of their awareness, so this difference may simply reflect the extent to which the teachers recognize how their own social identities shape their relationships with their students. Also, I did not explicitly ask about it during my interviews, but for teachers like Sadie who need to bridge cultural differences to effectively engage with students, they cannot describe their teaching without explaining how they manage that aspect of their teaching. In any case, it is worth reflecting on the ways we are like and unlike our students and how that shapes our relationships with them.

From Around the #MTBoS

Reflections on Being a White Teacher

Anne Schwartz teaches high school math in Southern California. I am excerpting a blog post of hers where she describes how she has come to make sense of being a white teacher for the diverse students in her school. Her point in sharing these conversations: Even if we, as white teachers, don't talk about our whiteness, our students of color still notice and it matters. Knowing who we are and how students perceive us allows us to be authentic with them.

It took me a lot of years to figure out I was white or at least to know it in any way that mattered. It took more than that for me to be able to talk about it in class. This snippet happened recently as part of a bigger conversation.

Me: *I didn't know I was white growing up.*

Student 1: *What do you mean you didn't know?*

Me: *Well, when did you know you were brown?*

Student 2: *Like, I don't know, always.*

Student 1: *I mean, seriously, like I never didn't know.*

Me: *No really, think, when was the first time you knew that you were brown?*

[Pause]

Student 2:   *I guess it was when my mom looked different than the other moms at kindergarten. I like knew those kids were white so I was not white.*

Student 1:   *Yeah, I mean I always noticed kids had different skin even when I was really little.*

Me: *OK, well I didn't know being white was even a thing till high school and I didn't realize it affected my life till I was probably twenty-six.*

I talk to kids about the way I grew up. I talk about the way people look at me in stores, the way I see myself reflected in TV and books, the things people assume about me because I am white. I talk about privilege. I use the word *privilege*. I tell them I have all sorts of privilege they don't: I'm an adult, I'm their teacher, and I'm white.

I have said this before and will say it again, I am not a magical wizard teacher. I do not do this perfectly all the time. I do not casually inform my children about racism in the perfectly modeled lesson with questions ready and responses prethought. I do though wade into waters that are tricky. I stumble and screw up and falter for the right words. I do not get through to every child. White boys are a particular challenge for me in these conversations.

I can say pretending that me being a white lady didn't matter wasn't effective. Thinking that the children might not notice I was white or trying not to notice they weren't (or were) did not lead to a realistic community in my classroom.

As the next chapters will describe, the featured teachers' practices, in all their wonderful variation, help create motivational mathematics classrooms by attending to belongingness, meaningfulness, competence, accountability, and autonomy. By understanding how different teachers design their classrooms to reduce social risk and invite student participation, others can be supported in revamping their instruction toward the same ends.

3 | Belongingness

Each child wants to know immediately if he is a worthy person in your eyes. You cannot pretend, because the child knows all the things about himself that worry him. If you act like you like him, but ignore the things he is anxious about, it doesn't count. The child is glad you are nice to him, but deep down he figures if you really knew what he was like, you'd hate him. So your liking him without knowing him just makes him feel guilty.

—VIVIAN PALEY, *WHITE TEACHER*

Mathematics education is identity work. Learners are always positioning themselves with respect to the doing of mathematics, their sense of themselves and their communities, and their futures.

—ROCHELLE GUTIÉRREZ, "THE SOCIOPOLITICAL TURN IN MATHEMATICS EDUCATION"

> **What Belongingness Means**

Many students enter mathematics classrooms with a sense of trepidation. For some, their discomfort reflects a larger sense of detachment from school. They may not feel welcomed because of the gaps they experience navigating between their home language or culture and the expectations at school. The social milieu of school may make them feel like an outcast, as they see peers who seamlessly "fit in" while they remain on the outside. Unlike the sports field, their community center, or the stage, academic settings may make them feel untalented and incompetent. For other students, school itself is fine, but there is a distinct dread upon entering math class. Math has never made sense—or it made sense when it involved whole numbers, but as soon as the variables showed up, all hope was lost. A standardized test score that deemed them "below grade level" may have demoralized them. They may get messages at home that "*we're* not good at math," setting up any potential success as familial disloyalty. For some students, they love the subject, but must contend with others who do not see them as fitting their ideas of "a math person." They have to combat stereotypes constantly to be seen as legitimate participant in the classroom, as they defy expectations.

For most students, teachers who create a sense of belongingness can overcome these forms of alienation. Belongingness comes about when students experience frequent, pleasant interactions with their peers and teacher. It also comes about with the sense that others are concerned for who they are and for their overall well-being. Like the Vivian Paley quote in the epigraph suggests, belongingness is fostered through authentic connections—seeing students for who they are, their strengths, their challenges, and accepting and embracing both as we work with them and help them grow. And as Rochelle Gutiérrez reminds us, connecting students and the content is fundamentally identity work, as we help students develop a sense of themselves and their own possibilities. In this chapter, I will describe common practices that prevent students from feeling like they belong in math class, and strategies for fostering a sense of belongingness.

> **Belongingness:** *When students experience frequent, pleasant interactions with the sense that others are concerned about who they are and for their well-being.*

> **Why Belongingness Matters**

When I observe in mathematics classrooms, I can usually gauge students' general sense of belongingness. What is their affect as they walk through the door? How warmly and personally do they greet the teacher and their classmates? How do they respond when they are asked to participate? Do they approach the teacher beyond formal instruction? Is there a sense of comfort and familiarity? Are they represented in what is posted on the walls, through math work or other means?

All too often, I see students enter their math classrooms with a sense of gloom. Smiles disappear as they cross the threshold of the doorway, as if a soul-sucking Dementor lurks in the doorway. Their posture slumps. They sit at the back of the room or put their heads on their desks. (See Rafranz Davis' "seat assessment" in Chapter 2.) They may even groan or launch into a litany of complaints. When I observe these behaviors as a teacher, it signals that I have work to do to make students feel welcome and comfortable spending their time learning mathematics with me.

Teachers' relationships with students are an important source of belongingness, but peers are equally (if not more) important. Even if a teacher welcomes each student with a smile and asks a question about how things are going, other students' insults or intimidation can contribute to a negative classroom climate. To support belongingness, then, teachers need to do more than forge strong relationships. They also need to establish and maintain clear norms and expectations about how students treat each other.

During adolescence, children face the task of developing a strong and stable sense of themselves. Although this identity development happens over the course of a lifetime, adolescence is distinct: it is when children are first able to think abstractly enough to grapple with both their own emerging self-understandings as well as how society views them. For many students, this leads to a delightful self-awareness and a sometimes-painful self-consciousness, leaving them more sensitive to others' perspectives and feedback. Necessarily then, inclusive and inviting classrooms provide a place for this crucial developmental work, particularly in relationship to school in general and mathematics in particular. Indeed, educational researchers have found belongingness to be critical to students' engagement and, ultimately, academic success (Booker and Lim 2016).

How Belongingness Shifts Social Risk

Recall that students perceive the social risk in the math classroom by weighing the relative costs against the possible benefits of participation. When students feel uncomfortable or marginalized, many of them prefer to avoid the scrutiny of their teacher and peers, using minimal participation as a safeguard against judgments. On the other hand, when they feel the emotional safety that comes with belongingness, they are inclined to take risks, knowing that the fundamental acceptance of who they are outweighs what might happen in a particular moment.

Relationships and caring are so critical, even a simple identification between teacher and student can pay academic dividends. Psychologist Hunter Gehlbach and his colleagues found that when they helped teachers and students identify similarities with each other, the teachers perceived better relationships with those students, and, in turn, the students earned higher class grades. Their small intervention of finding commonalities significantly narrowed achievement disparities between students (Gehlbach et al. 2016).

> What Gets in the Way of Belongingness

When school proceeds as usual, without even intending it, teachers may interact with students in ways that are experienced as *rejecting*. Rejecting interactions communicate to students that they are not welcome or valued. They span a wide range, from the inadvertent (e.g., forgetting a student's name) to the commonplace (e.g., harsh feedback on work) to the egregious (e.g., a bald insult). More generally, teachers engage in rejecting interactions when they devalue who students are. This happens in many ways, some of which teachers may not realize. For instance, some teachers avoid using what is for them an unfamiliar and "difficult-to-pronounce" name. Not only does this lead to fewer invitations for that student to participate, it communicates that the teacher is not comfortable with something that marks the child's difference. Names are deeply personal, one of the first words we identify with, and they often reflect our home cultures and personal history. When teachers avoid them or change them without consent, they devalue something core to who students are (Kohli and Solórzano 2012).

Likewise, when teachers problematically differentiate their treatment of students based on cultural expectations, they devalue who students are. Educational researcher Ebony McGee studies successful students of color in science, technology, engineering, and mathematics (STEM) fields. She interviewed a Black chemistry major at a historically White institution who reported that a White instructor avoided her when she dressed in a way often perceived by middle-class teachers as "ghetto." When the student changed her clothing style, the teacher told her, "Now you actually look presentable. I bet you are making better grades too" (McGee 2016). Similarly, in a research project I conducted, after a math teacher emailed a student's mother to complain that the student's skirts were too short, the girl concluded that her teacher didn't like her (Horn 2008). Adolescents use clothing to express themselves, their gender, and their culture as a part of the identity work they engage in. Avoiding, judging, or rejecting them because of these forms of self-expression can further estrange them from the classroom or school. Communicating a school's dress code expectations while maintaining respect for students' self-expression is an important relational skill for teachers to develop.

Additionally, teachers may alienate students by correcting the inconsequential. Although our job involves helping students to become educated people, when we correct the inconsequential, we often work against other goals of engagement and inclusion. Deciding what is inconsequential is, of course, a judgment call: context is everything. To illustrate with a more obvious example, our standards for speech and language differ when students try to explain an idea they are grappling with versus when they are preparing for a job interview. In the former situation, correct grammar is not the point, and in the second, it matters a lot. If our students are learning English as a second language, speaking a pidgin, or using African American Vernacular English, our focus on correct grammar when it is inconsequential may disinvite their participation. To take a math-specific example, in a class discussion about a new and challenging concept, a student's (or teacher's!) miscalculation should not be overemphasized. We all make missteps, and this rough draft talk (see Mercer and Hodgkinson 2008) should be normalized to focus on the main instructional point. When students feel like their good efforts are met with nitpicking, it can discourage their participation.

Finally, teachers alienate students by having narrow ideas about on-task behavior. For some teachers, a successful lesson is one where every student is on-task, meaning they are all doing their work quietly, without interruptions or side talk. However, this kind of on-task, compliant behavior is not necessarily the same as engaged learning. As mathematics education researcher Jo Boaler (2002) has described, students can be engaged in learning important mathematics while drifting seamlessly between schoolish mathematics and social activity. In her study, many students who looked off-task actually engaged deeply in the mathematics, with no detriment (and many benefits) to their mathematical learning. When teachers emphasize on-task behavior over authentic engagement, they force students to choose between acting the part of a student, which may feel false, and being their full selves, which may include being playful, silly, or simply interested in the social lives of their peers.

Classroom Climate

Beyond the teacher-student relationship, different classroom climates can work against a sense of belongingness. For instance, many math classrooms emphasize *competition*.

Whether this comes from formal races, timed tests, or just students' informal comparison of grades, competition sends a strong message that some people are more mathematically able than others. This is problematic because there is typically one kind of smartness that leads students to win these competitions: quick and accurate calculation. To paraphrase mathematician John Allen Paulos (1991), nobody tells you that you cannot be a writer because you are not a fast typist; yet we regularly communicate to students that they cannot be mathematicians because they do not compute quickly. (In Chapter 5, I will describe more fully how mathematics draws on different forms of smartness, so this narrow idea of mathematics ability does not accurately reflect the discipline.) Although a competitive dynamic may be at play in other school subjects, it is especially toxic in math classrooms because students do not have other venues to explore and affirm their diverse mathematical talents. Stakes are high: students' access to advanced mathematics in the middle grades shapes their educational access as they move on to high school (McGraw et al. 2006).

Finally, groups of disaffected peers can sometimes cluster together in a classroom, withdrawing from activities as a group. Through their influence over others, they can set a negative tone for the rest of the class and increase the social risk of participation by forming an alternative set of "standards" by which student involvement is judged. Although teachers may be inclined to break up the group or coerce them into desired behavior, this approach can backfire. Instead, the teacher needs to work to reengage the group and help them feel like they are a part of the classroom community. Sometimes, students coalesce against the teacher as a symptom of general mistrust between the adults and students in a school. This requires a broader intervention, with the cooperation of colleagues and administrators.

> Strategies for Fostering Belongingness

The featured teachers have a few primary strategies for creating a sense of belongingness in their mathematics classrooms. First, the organization of the physical space should be welcoming and inclusive. Second, teachers deliberately support both their relationships with students and students' relationships with each other to make an environment conducive to frequent, positive interactions and a prevailing sense of caring. Additionally, they develop routines that emphasize cooperation, infusing instructional interactions with a sense of belongingness. Finally, they advocate for children who are experiencing rejection from the school itself.

Organizing Physical Space

We all have had the experience of a welcoming environment, a place you walk into and feel a sense of comfort. Although the featured teachers work in a range of school settings with varying resources, they make an effort to create inviting classroom spaces. Some teachers do this by giving their students space in the classroom to express themselves. For instance, Rafranz Davis had a Not-Math Wall. She described it like "their own refrigerator" where students could hang things that were personally meaningful to them. Students would hang sports pictures, drawings, or pictures of their children. "If they doodled in class that day, the students put it on the wall," Rafranz explained. "I wanted my classroom to be a place where they all felt it was theirs." Similarly, Peg Cagle dedicated a space in her classroom for students, called the Truth Wall. At the top, a banner read, "We Hold These Truths to Be Self-Evident." Peg put up posters affirming lesbian, gay, bisexual, transgender, and queer (LGBTQ) youth and sending antibullying messages. The students' postings ranged from silly (e.g., fortune cookie messages) to personally meaningful (e.g., opinions on the designated hitter rule in American League baseball) to reflections of their cultural heritage. Considering the identity work that happens in adolescence, these boards provided spaces for students to represent themselves in ways not typically invited in math class. In exchange, the teachers had a wider lens on who students were and what they valued.

Other signs around the classroom communicate belongingness to students. Sadie Estrella drew a picture in the corner of her whiteboard: two stick people labeled "Ms. Sadie and YOU," with two arrows going toward each other. She told her students, "Remember this picture. This is our deal. I will meet you but I am not doing it all. You have to meet me too." This constant reminder of Sadie's care for her students served as an emblem of belongingness, communicating her investment in them, along with her expectations for mutual commitment.

Aside from wall decor, seating arrangements can convey a sense of inclusion. For example, Rafranz arranged her desks in such a way that there was no back of the room. "Some kids sit in the back because they don't want anything to do with the teacher. Some sit in the back because they think they are bad at math." By arranging her desks in a circle where students faced each other and circulating around as she taught, Rafranz established during the first weeks of school that all students needed to participate—and equally important, that all students belonged. Of course, some classrooms are too crowded or desks immobile, limiting possible seating arrangements. You might allow students to circulate during classwork or rotate seating arrangements at regular intervals to prevent students from becoming entrenched in their back-of-the-class positions.

Ideas from the #MTBoS

Megan Schmidt's Dog Wall

Megan Schmidt's love of dogs—especially beagles—is no secret to anybody who meets her or who reads her blog, *Number Loving Beagle*. She shares this affection with her students on her Dog Wall. On it, students can post pictures of their dogs, dogs they think are cute, or, as one sassy student chose, Snoop Dogg. Students often enter her class, see the dog wall, and relax with a smile. Younger siblings of former students will say, "Hey! You have a picture of my dog on the wall!" In Megan's class, the Dog Wall allows the teacher and students to find something in common.

Too often, in our focus on methods and techniques, we can overlook the significance of the physical environment and the messages it sends to students. Our choices about what we post on the walls and how we set up the space can make our classrooms welcoming places for our students.

Building Relationships

Because belongingness comes from frequent, pleasant interactions and a sense of caring concern, relationships are at the heart of belongingness. Most teachers recognize the importance of building relationships with students. Research has shown the importance of this human connection, with desirable academic outcomes significantly and positively related to strong teacher-student relationships (Gehlbach et al. 2012). As Rafranz told me, "It doesn't matter, you can be the best teacher on earth in terms of content. If you cannot reach those kids to the heart of who they are, you're not going to reach them."

Chris Luzniak sets out to connect with students immediately. To facilitate this, on the first day of class, he has students fill out a note card with their name, cell phone number, best person to contact at home, how to contact them, and three things about themselves. "By the second day," he told me, "I know all their names. I have their pictures so I can go home and study if I am a little unsure." Notice that this groundwork for relationship building extends to his students' families too. Knowing how to contact them, developing systems for communication, and building positive relationships are all key to helping students develop a sense of belonging.

In addition to getting to know the basics, Chris' first assignment for his students is to write a "mathography," two paragraphs about themselves and their math experiences. "They have to email it to me, then I email them back." He writes a short paragraph back to let students know that he has read what they wrote. The exchange not only sets a further foundation for their relationship, it provides him with a record of *who* particular students are, so if they email him later on, he has an easily retrievable record.

Ideas from the #MTBoS

Sara Van Der Werf's Name Tents with Feedback

On the first day of class, Sara Van Der Werf projects a slide asking students to find their seat and fold a 5 × 8-inch card into a name tent. On the outside, she wants them to write their name on both sides, so both she and their peers can begin to learn everyone's names. Inside the card, she has already printed a "first week feedback form" that looks like this:

Name:

Use this form to communicate with me. Write a comment OR question OR make a suggestion about this class. (Ideally a couple of sentences). **Each day I will respond to whatever you write. Thank you for your time. Leave this name tent on your table each day.**

POSSIBLE QUESTIONS TO RESPOND TO: How do you feel about math? What would you like me to know about you outside of school? What hopes do you have for this class (Advanced Algebra) for 2016-17? What do you like about math or this class? What are you fearful of? What activities (sports/arts/jobs…) are you involved in after school? Draw a picture/sketch of how you are feeling. Draw a picture/sketch of something that represents you.

Monday, August 29	Tuesday, August 30	Wednesday, August 31	Thursday, September 1	Friday, September 2
Comments: (student)	Comments:	Comments:	Ask me a question:	Comments:
Response: (teacher)	Response:	Response:	Response:	Response:

Reprinted with permission from Sara Van Der Werf.

Sara lets her students know that they are expected to learn everybody's name by the end of the week. She has them start by learning the names of people at their table, asking them to learn five new names by the end of the day.

During the first week, each day, at the end of class, she gives students a moment to write her a note inside their name tents. At the end of the day, she takes a moment to write a note back to each and every one as a way of establishing her relationship.

Day 1	Day 2	Day 3	Day 4	Day 5
Comments (student): it was a good day today. I like the numbers that tells us something about us. I miss Algebra because I had Ms. T. Do you know her?	Comments: the video we watched was funny and very interesting to know that is how we look if we don't try to get to class ahead.	Comments: i liked the group activity. It was fun.	Comments: that groupwork was frusterating but it makes me want to find the answer. Is there more funny stories about your nephews?	Comments: i hope you had a good first week!
Response (teacher): I do know Ms. T! She is awesome. Lucky you.	Response: I like this video a lot. If I am honest, I look as foolish as those people sometimes! ☺	Response: Good to hear! My goal is to do something fun at least once in awhile.	Response: I will bring some in when they do crazy stuff!!	Response: Thanks! You too! ☺

Reprinted with permission from Sara Van Der Werf.

Sara reports that she learns a lot about her students from these exchanges. She acknowledges that this process takes a lot of time, but, she writes, "This was totally worth the time I spent on the them." She even went back to the name tents a month or so later and found more clues about who her students were: their strengths, their questions, and their concerns.

Sadie knew how important it was for her to welcome her students to her *math* classroom, a place where they have often been made to feel incompetent or unsure.

> *I know my kids weren't always really good at math—there's not a lot of people that are not. But I got to see them at the community softball game, and I got to see their strengths. I got to see them with their family. I'd see them taking care of their brothers and sisters. I get to see them personally and that they excel in something and I like to engage in conversations with them about that. Because I know that you might not be the best in math but you're good at something.*

By recognizing these outside strengths, Sadie let her students know that she saw them as whole people, giving them the confidence to take risks with her teaching. Sadie also attributes her success in helping her students open up to the authenticity of their relationships. "When I started creating that safe environment, you see that they start talking. You see that they are talking about math, then they start talking about life . . . they'll talk about anything, you know, and you can talk to them like real people." Adolescents tend to have a great nose for phoniness, so figuring out how to create those connections while being yourself is critical.

Some teachers put students at ease by sharing things about themselves. Fawn Nguyen's students knew certain facts about her from the start—especially her love of the University of Oregon Ducks. They teased her about the team's losses, cheered for her when they succeeded, and even surprised her by dressing in green, the team color. By sharing her passions, she made a place for students to share themselves. Fawn's playfulness and affection is contagious. When she describes her relationships with her students, she says, "We laugh a lot, and I tell them how much I love them all the time." The warm environment Fawn created in her classroom not only sustained the students' engagement, but her own as well. "I have so much fun with the kids. If I didn't, I would have quit teaching long ago. Sure, I love to sleep in too. But they're my kids. They're my family." She has her limits though: "We can talk all day, you know, and the kids love it. They've asked me random questions about my life and interests. I mean, they genuinely have interesting questions." At a certain point, she needs to defer their curiosity, and she tells them, "Come in at lunch. We'll talk more during lunch. But not during class time. There's a time for everything."

Check Your Biases

We *all* have biases. It is part of being human. Our unconscious biases come into play even more when we are hurried to make decisions. Because teachers have been estimated to make over a thousand decisions a day, there are plenty of opportunities for unconscious bias to come into play. If you have noticed certain patterns in your classroom—girls speak more than boys, students of color are disciplined more frequently than White students—it may be useful to examine how you might be contributing to these situations. Project Implicit (http://www.projectimplicit.net) provides a free web tool that allows you to examine different unconscious biases that might be contributing to your own decisions. The anonymous results are shared with researchers. I took some of the tests and found it fascinating to learn about my own biases. That is how we all get better.

Routines and Structures

Although we typically think of classroom routines and structures as ways of holding students accountable (see Chapter 6), they can also invite belongingness. One way is through routines that provide ways for teachers to connect to students' home languages and cultures. By providing discourse structures that invite students to make sense of mathematics in their own language, teachers make spaces for that aspect of students' identities in their classrooms. Elizabeth Statmore finds such opportunities when her students are using Talking Points. "I find that listening and doing Talking Points often gives me an opportunity to connect with kids whose cultures are very different from mine," she told me. "I try to be receptive and respectful of their cultural needs, so if someone is very, very quiet or reserved and is not comfortable speaking up in groups, they can sort of get in and get out without betraying their own ideas about what is expected of them." In other classrooms I have visited, collaborative group structures have supported students speaking in their home language, without concerns about communicating to the whole class in English.

Routines and structures can also provide a sense of belonging by making spaces for students' selves. At their most effective, the structures point students' activities toward mathematical ideas while providing latitude for self-expression. There is, of course, vulnerability that comes from exposing one's true self in this way. As Elizabeth explains, "Being authentic in public means allowing yourself to feel vulnerable. You have to teach them how to be vulnerable in the ways that are psychologically, emotionally safe." The Counting Circles, Talking Points, Visual Patterns, and Math Debates structures (see Chapter 2) all have openings for students' input and ideas while providing enough supports to guard against these vulnerabilities.

Advocating for Students

Sometimes, when teachers open their classrooms and their hearts to make a place for alienated students, they become their allies in a system that has not welcomed them. Rafranz had a powerful experience with one such student. "I had a student who completely changed everything, and reaffirmed why I came into teaching anyway." She had connected with him in her eighth-grade class and saw him slipping through the cracks, with gang involvement and the school's lack of concern. After he was stabbed in the hallway, she called his house to check on how he was doing. "I remember him coming back and he's like, 'You called my house.' He said, 'Why did you call my house?' I said, 'You weren't in school.' He said, 'Well nobody else called.' I said, 'Well, clearly I'm not anybody else.'"

From that point forward, he opened up to her. "It was indescribable, the things that he would describe to me that he saw starting when he was five years old." She soon figured out that he was dyslexic and had not been receiving services for his disability. When the counselors helped him determine his high school schedule, they pushed him out of academic classes, despite his personal goal to become a physician. He came to her in tears. "That day he was broken and that was the day when I said, 'Alright, Rafranz. If and when the job opens at the high school, you need to do it.'" And she did, seeing him through to graduation, continuing her role as his advocate.

When I was teaching high school, a colleague and I worked together to move our students through the curricular pipeline. Between us, we covered the early course sequence, and we would, for example, switch students from prealgebra to algebra midyear if needed, with a transitional plan for support and extra tutoring. We saw a lot of students being placed in courses that were not challenging enough, or students who would suddenly find a new commitment in their academic work and show an ability to catch up to grade level. Disproportionately, these students came from low-income homes or racial groups that have been historically disenfranchised from U.S. schools. Mathematics education researcher Rochelle Gutiérrez (1996) describes such teacher workarounds as strategies that *organize for advancement*, where we deliberately work against the grain of schooling structures that keep students out of the college preparatory pipeline. Developing a critical eye toward schooling structures that push out our students—what Gutiérrez (2013) calls the political knowledge for mathematics teaching—is an important part of being their advocates.

Belongingness Audit

1. What is the physical space of your room? How is it organized? Is it welcoming? What messages does it send about students—who they are, what matters in your class, what it means to be smart, what it means to be a good citizen of your classroom? What opportunities are there for access to different space and movement in your classroom?

2. How do you learn students' names? Teach them each other's names?

3. What do you do to get to know your students beyond math class? How do you welcome them? How do you connect to their families?

4. Think of a student whose participation concerns you. What do you know about this student's:

   - academic history in math
   - socioeconomic status
   - family situation
   - nationality
   - transience (prior schools, foster status, homelessness)
   - parents' or guardians' jobs
   - home responsibilities
   - after-school work commitments
   - religious affiliation
   - home languages
   - home technology access
   - personal interests (sports, music, television, movies, books, hobbies, arts)
   - physical health
   - history of behavior or discipline concerns
   - socioemotional learning strengths and challenges
   - existence of individualized education plan or a 504 plan
   - challenges such as Tourette syndrome, Asperger syndrome, attention-deficit hyperactivity disorder
   - vision or hearing problems
   - gifted/advanced learner identification
   - LGBTQ identity and transitions

5. How might these different aspects of your students' experience contribute to or inhibit their sense of belonging in your classroom?

6. What schooling practices do you engage in that might impede belongingness (e.g., competition, correcting the inconsequential, emphasizing being on-task rather than engaged)?

7. How do you set a tone of respect among the students themselves?

8. How do you respond to students' noncompliance with structures and routines? When students are late, forget homework, or do not study, do you go into "teacher mode" and scold them? Or do you work to learn why these things have happened and solve the problem together?

9. How do you balance supporting students' self-expression with your school's dress code?

10. How do you reach out to students' families and communities? How do you keep the lines of communication open at key moments (around report cards, when you note a change in a student's behavior)?

4 | Meaningfulness

Learning is not just about "correcting" what students already know. Learning is not just about students' acquiring what some in schools and society have already determined to be the things that they are "supposed" to know. Given the recognition that curriculum cannot help but be partial, learning needs to involve refusing to be comfortable with what we already know and what we are coming to know.

—KEVIN KUMASHIRO, "TOWARD A THEORY OF
ANTI-OPPRESSIVE EDUCATION"

The beauty of mathematics only shows itself to more patient followers.

—MARYAM MIRZAKHANI, IN "MARYAM MIRZAKHANI:
'THE MORE I SPENT TIME ON MATHS, THE MORE EXCITED I GOT'"

> What Meaningfulness Means

Learning and schooling are not the same thing. There are children who are great learners but terrible students. These young people are full of ideas and questions, but they have not managed to connect their innate curiosity with their experiences in school. There are many possible reasons for this. As discussed in the previous chapter, children may find school to be a hard place to inhabit, due to invisible expectations that leave them feeling alienated. Sometimes, school curriculum just seems irrelevant. As Kevin Kumashiro (2012) acknowledges in the quote at the start of this chapter, children's questions about the world do not always find inroads in the work they are asked to do in school.

Although many parenting books extol children's natural curiosity and emphasize its importance in their learning and development, schooling too often emphasizes compliance over curiosity. Thus, it is not surprising that children who are great learners and weak students have their antithesis: children who are *great students* but who are less invested in learning and sense making. Make no mistake: these students hit every mark of good organization, diligence, and timely work production, but they do not seek deep engagement with academic content. Given the freedom to develop a question or explore an idea, they balk and ask for more explicit directions. I have heard teachers refer to such children as "teacher-dependent." As the following image illustrates, these two types of children lie at extremes, highlighting inherent tensions between learning and schooling.

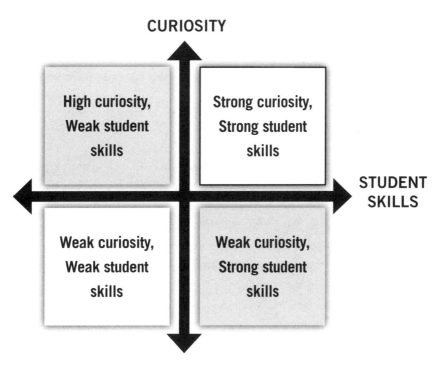

Tensions between *learning* and *schooling,* as illustrated by children's academic curiosity and student skills. Children on the right tend to do well in school.

Too often, *meaningfulness* falls through the gap between learning and schooling. There is a fundamental contradiction at play: meaningfulness arises from and connects to children's curiosity, yet "curious children" is not entirely synonymous with "successful students."

Meaningfulness comes about when students develop an appreciation for mathematical ideas. Rich learning happens when students draw on prior knowledge and experiences to make sense of ideas and explore problems, invoke their own strategies, get to ask their own "what if" questions. In short, meaningful learning happens when students' activity connects to their own curiosity.

To make meaningfulness central to math teaching, then, teachers need to narrow the gap between *being curious* and *being a good student.* Referring to the previous illustration, we want to design classrooms that move as many children into the top right quadrant as we can: we want to create structures that help them to be successful students, *and* we want to engage their curiosity.

> **Meaningfulness**: *When students connect their own curiosity and experience to ideas, thereby developing an interest in and appreciation for mathematical content.*

> Why Meaningfulness Matters

Every math teacher, at one time or another, has been asked, "When are we going to use this?" Although this question often gets cast as students' resistance to learning, it can be productively reinterpreted as a plea for meaningfulness. When the hidden curriculum of math class—the messages that are inadvertently relayed through classroom organization and activity—consistently communicates that meaning does *not* matter, we end up with hordes of students who no longer reason when they are doing math. Instead, they focus on *rituals* and *cues* (see pp. 48–51 for more on these).

As researcher Sheila Tobias (1990) explained in her classic exploration of math anxiety, this lack of meaning exacerbates many students' negative experiences learning mathematics. When math class emphasizes rituals and cues that rely on memorization and compliance over sense making, students' own interpretations get devalued. For instance, students memorize multiplication facts, and, in a search for meaning, they decide *that multiplication makes things bigger.* Then, they learn how to multiply numbers between 0 and 1. Their prior understanding of multiplication no longer works, so they might settle on the idea that *multiplication intensifies numbers,* because it makes these fractional quantities even smaller. Finally, when they learn how to multiply negative numbers, all these attempts to make sense of multiplication fall apart and become meaningless, leaving them completely at sea. The inability to make sense of procedures leaves students grasping and anxious, as the procedures seem ever more arbitrary, making failure seem likely and incompetence inevitable.

In contrast, when classrooms focus on mathematical sense making, they reap multiple motivational benefits. Students' ownership over their learning increases. Reimagining the prior example, students see that multiplication can be thought of as repeated addition, the dimensions of a rectangle related to its area, or the inverse of division. With this foundation, when they learn multiplication of new types of numbers, the answers stand to make sense, because they have concepts to expand on. This, in turn, makes their learning more durable. Furthermore, when students understand the meaning behind the mathematics they are learning, they are more likely to connect it to their own experiences, providing openings for their own curiosity and questions. In this way, meaningful mathematics classrooms provide students chances to identify and explore their own problems.

Exploring one's own questions pays dividends for learning. In a systematic comparison of teacher-guided and student-driven problem solving, educational researchers Tesha Sengupta-Irving and Noel Enyedy (2014) found that the ownership, relevance, and opportunities to engage curiosity in student-driven problem solving supported stronger outcomes in student affect and engagement. Other researchers have linked meaningful mathematics learning to the long-term persistence among students from nondominant groups (Herzig 2002).

How Meaningfulness Shifts Social Risk

There are many reasons why students are reluctant to participate in math class. They are distracted. They have had six classes since they last sat in our room. They are not even sure what happened in the last class session. They are hungry, worried, heartbroken, tired. These reasons alone can shift their risk-taking calculus: when they weigh the social risks and benefits of participation, on the balance, they are not compelled to publicly engage.

The situation is harder when a gulf exists between schooling and learning. The students described as inhabiting the extremes of this contradiction are particularly vulnerable. For children driven by their curiosity, ritualistic math classrooms are socially risky, because success in math does not line up with their own need to make sense of the world, instead emphasizing compliance and following what often seem like arbitrary rules. For these children, participation would be most satisfying if they had a chance to engage their own questions, but many mathematics classrooms are not designed to support this.

On the other extreme, young people committed to being "good" students (but not especially connected to their academic curiosity) willingly participate in ritualistic math classrooms—*if* they feel fairly certain about the cues. As soon as questions become open ended and demanding, however, they often balk, feeling more comfortable with the demands of rituals like remembering and applying the most recently used procedure or definition. For these students, pleasing the teacher or earning a good grade are the primary benefits of participation.

Both groups of students need serious support to participate meaningfully. The first group needs clear indications that the rules of classroom engagement support their curiosity, as well as guidance in how to participate effectively as students. The second group requires assurances that they can competently participate, even without the usual rituals and cues. (See Chapter 5 on competence for more on this issue.) Teachers need to actively support students in making the shift to meaningful learning. Many students feel safe with the low-risk demands of remembering and applying as they work on familiar tasks. Novel mathematical tasks, although they support meaning making, are riskier because solution paths are not clear. This ambiguity leaves more openings for students to feel unsure or, even worse, stupid. Many classroom routines and structures need to be reworked to support students with these new ways of mathematical engagement. If our questions, tasks, and activities support sense making, over time, they can gain confidence that their own logic and experience will legitimately contribute to the discussion and may even discover their own intellectual curiosities.

> What Gets in the Way of Meaningfulness

Math class rituals align more to the structure of schooling than they align to developing meaningful understanding. Responding to the demands of curriculum coverage and the inevitable crowds teachers contend with, most classrooms are structured for high-volume work production instead of meaningful learning. As educational researcher Walter Doyle (1988) described in his study of such "production classes," these classrooms share a number of characteristics:

> *Content was divided in small chunks, instruction was stepwise, progress through the curriculum was rapid and efficient. In addition, there was often little differential weighting of credit for different tasks. All tasks were equal, and final-*

term grades were calculated by averaging grades on individual tasks. Finally tasks in production classes were often interchangeable. That is, although there may have been a broad sequence (e.g., addition before multiplication or fractions before decimals), the ordering of tasks for a day or a week was somewhat arbitrary. Decisions about the order of tasks were based, it appears, on management considerations, personal preferences, or perceived motivational requirements, rather than a logical or semantic thread that might have tied the separate tasks together. (175)

Work production classes adapt to the demands of schooling, but they do not fully support students' meaning making. The absence of "a logical or semantic thread" points to inattention to making sense of what was being learned. Although these structures allow students to march through a lot of content—what teachers often call "coverage"—and produce high volumes of work, they get few opportunities to grapple with meaning, let alone relate it to their lives. When teachers dole out content in mostly undifferentiated chunks, they take away these opportunities from students. The unnatural evenness of the curriculum and the lack of a semantic thread devalue sense-making questions like, "How is this like what we learned before? How is it different? Why?" Yet such questions aid students in developing the connected understandings that are at the heart of meaningful learning. Additionally, the emphasis on work production reinforces the problematic idea that, if a student understands what is being taught, math problems should be solvable quickly, discouraging the deep engagement required for mathematical problem solving (Schoenfeld 1988).

Rituals

In classrooms organized for work production, some well-established math class rituals emerge. One of the best documented involves looking at an example and then doing the same thing with increasing order of difficulty (Stigler and Hiebert 2009). For instance, in a lesson on solving two-step linear equations, a teacher might demonstrate the solution to:

$$7x - 3 = 18$$

and then have students work independently on twenty similar problems, with the teacher circulating around the room to assist when they get stuck. Maybe students work in pairs, coaching each other on the steps. Because the problems get harder as they progress, they require increasingly complicated calculations with negative divisors or noninteger solutions. The procedural question of *how* animates this ritual much more than the sense-making question of *why.*

After engaging in procedure-driven rituals over time, many students internalize what ıcational researchers James Stigler and James Hiebert (2009) call a "cultural script" for math class: to succeed, they primarily need to learn terms and practice procedures. Note that by avoiding the *why* question, these rituals circumvent meaning. Instead, students follow algorithms ("You get rid of the 3 to isolate the $7x$"), bypassing the underlying mathematical ideas, such as using inverse operations to isolate the variable or pressing on what it means to solve for an unknown quantity. Shortchanging this reasoning, in turn, diminishes students' future mathematical sense making. For instance, if students truly made sense of how they were using inverse operations to solve the two-step equations with multiplying and addition, they could predict how to solve a different kind of two-step equation: $x^2 - 10 = 15$. They would have a basis for understanding why this new equation has two solutions instead of one. Unfortunately, the ritual of practicing procedures limits robust sense making.

Cues

In work production classes, students' participation is organized around efficiency, compliance, and curricular coverage. This leads to cue-based reasoning, another common way students sidestep meaning making in math class. When asked to do an unfamiliar task, students often do not reason by making sense of the problem, but instead, they look for cues in the logic of the classroom. Sometimes, students use teacher cues, scrutinizing the teacher's facial expressions or verbal responses to ascertain the correctness of their answers. Other times, students use prior lesson cues and assume that a nonstandard problem will, like most other problems, simply require an application of whatever they have just been learning. Although this is an adaptive strategy in many work production classrooms, it can lead students to struggle to make sense of nonroutine situations.

For instance, after a lesson on two-step equations, a teacher might ask a conceptual question like:

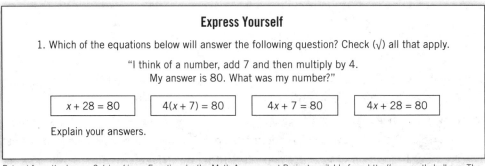

Express Yourself

1. Which of the equations below will answer the following question? Check (√) all that apply.

"I think of a number, add 7 and then multiply by 4.
My answer is 80. What was my number?"

| $x + 28 = 80$ | $4(x + 7) = 80$ | $4x + 7 = 80$ | $4x + 28 = 80$ |

Explain your answers.

Extract from the lesson *Solving Linear Equations* by the Math Assessment Project available from http://map.mathshell.org. The full lesson includes guidance on formative assessment and collaborative activities that tackle mistakes and misconceptions exposed by this starter task. Copyright © 2015 MARS, Shell Center, University of Nottingham. Reprinted by permission.

This interpretive question requires students to understand the meaning of the notation as they translate from English to math. If they have not made sense of what equations mean, they may go down the wrong path. If students work this problem using prior lesson cues, for instance, they simply apply the previously learned procedure to get "an answer" for each equation. This procedural approach is nonsensical in light of the particular question, but almost every math teacher I know has seen students uncritically apply the class' most recent procedure to the current question, no matter what is being asked. From the students' perspective, they "know" how to solve these kinds of problems, because they have done so twenty times on yesterday's worksheet. However, interpretive questions demand sense making, and the cultural script they are applying—which has often served them well as *students*—is maladaptive to this problem—which tries to engage them as *learners*. Old habits are thus an obstacle for teachers trying to make meaningful math learning the norm in their classrooms by bringing being curious and being a good student into closer proximity.

> Strategies for Creating Meaningful Learning

The featured math teachers use a few primary strategies to close the gap between being curious and being a student and to support meaningful learning. First, they set up inviting problems and structures that pique and draw out students' interest. Second, they make spaces in their instruction that invite students' curiosity and ideas. Finally, they develop ways to find interesting problems with their students.

Setting Up Inviting Problems

Peg Cagle often uses Playful Problems to invite her middle school students to play with mathematics. Her goal is to give her students something that, to them, is worth talking about. For example, to model simultaneous equations, she had students compare the rates of windup toys. Working in pairs, the students put, say, a windup baby and a windup Godzilla on opposite sides of a strip of paper. They then have to predict when the baby and Godzilla would collide. Recall that Peg aims for a climate of conjecturing in her classroom, so she wants to present problem situations that invite *what if* questions. The windup toy problem has many natural extensions: different toys traveling at different rates; the same toys on longer strips of paper. By varying the conditions, students are pressed to make generalizations about rate and distance as they make sense of simultaneous equations. Describing her problem designs, Peg explains, "Tasks have to be at least intriguing—if not out-and-out silly—so the kids would bother to get into them."

As she facilitates this conjecturing and problem solving, Peg has a few strategies for questioning students' activities. First, she never says anything a student can say. If she comes by a group and sees that a student understands enough to explain what is going on, she would rather support that student's emergent, rough draft explanation than provide a clean one herself. This provides a place for students' sense making. Second, she tries to phrase her questions to support students' interpretations, rather than just getting information. For example, to answer when Baby and Godzilla will collide, she avoids information questions like, "What is the solution?" Instead, she asks interpretive questions like, "What could we do to find the solution? How would you decide what might be the best way?" Although every lesson does not consist of Playful Problems, Peg describes them as touchstone experiences—memorable events that she can refer back to throughout the unit. In lessons following the windup toy exploration, for instance, Peg can show students another set of simultaneous equations and ask what would be happening if these were windup toys. In contrast to the undifferentiated tasks that characterize work production classes, touchstone experiences provide unique and engaging activities that anchor students' ongoing mathematical sense making.

Although they may seem quite different at first, Fawn Nguyen's Visual Pattern routine has a lot in common with Playful Problems. (See Chapter 2 for a full description.) The patterns are often intriguing and similarly invite students to wonder, predict, and conjecture about what is happening. They can ask *what if* questions, imagining how variations in the pattern would change their quantification of it. In this way, both Playful Problems and Visual Patterns provide an engaging entry point into doing meaningful mathematics. They share what mathematics educators often call *low floor/high ceiling* design (see, for example, Youcubed at Stanford University 2016). That is, they give students an easy entry into the mathematical situation because they are intuitive and accessible questions, but, at the same time, the contexts can be mined for rich mathematics. With Playful Problems, the tasks are deep enough to anchor a series of lessons as a touchstone experience. With Visual Patterns, students can learn, over time, how to mathematically interpret a wide range of patterns and model them with variables, a key understanding in middle school math. Both of inviting problems allow students to make meaning of mathematics, within and beyo lesson. Unlike tasks in work production classes, a semantic thread emerges as students reter to previous days' work and the strategies they remember.

Ideas from the #MTBoS

Dan Meyer: "If this skill is aspirin, how do I create the headache?"

Dan Meyer reminds us that mathematicians create mathematics to fulfill a need. One strategy for creating meaning is to help students see that need. For example, we can ask students to look at a field of dots, choose one, and then try to describe which one they selected to a partner:

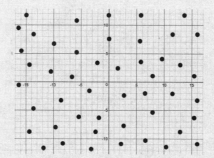

After letting them struggle with this task, we have created a headache for which coordinate planes are a cure.

When given the same challenge with a grid, students understand how the skill of naming points using the coordinate system alleviates the headache of naming points in space.

Making Spaces for Students' Ideas

Although low floor/high ceiling problems provide an entrée for students, there are other ways to help bridge the learning-schooling gap. Some teachers use discourse structures to scaffold participation in ways that lower social risk while making space for students' mathematical ideas. As described in Chapter 2, Sadie Estrella uses Counting Circles, Chris Luzniak uses Math Debates, and Elizabeth Statmore uses Talking Points. All of these structures deemphasize right or wrong answers and value students' ideas and support sense making.

In Chris' debate structure, he presents mathematical situations that have some degree of ambiguity, inviting students' opinions. For example, he might present an equation and ask for a sensible first step in solving it. He might present a system of equations and ask whether substitution, graphing, or elimination would be the best strategy. "They're eager to do the problems for me when it's more opinion, even though they are doing the math," he told me. "And I love that they are, in fact, doing a math problem. They're analyzing different possibilities for doing it, different ways to make mistakes." Math Debates also require students to listen to each other, because the structure obliges students to summarize in one sentence what a previous speaker has said.

Elizabeth's Talking Points discourse structure similarly sets students up to interpret mathematical situations. The structure lowers the social risk of explaining mathematical thinking by explicitly building in a place for students to change their minds, making this an expected part of their sense making. As Elizabeth described, through Talking Points, "Changing your mind becomes a classroom practice." Given the social risk typically associated with changing one's mind, this goes a long way toward closing the gaps between learning and schooling.

These discourse structures close the gap between learning and schooling in important ways. The structures provide the teachers a way to introduce ambiguity and demand interpretation, but they do so in ways that support students in taking the necessary risks. In addition, they emphasize students listening to each other, not the teacher, thus moving students into sense making and away from cue-based reasoning.

Problematizing: Finding Problems Together

Along with many of the other featured teachers, Rafranz Davis and Fawn Nguyen work hard to help students *see* mathematics in their environments. As Rafranz told me, "A good teacher looks for the math in students' lives. It was important to talk about the math that they encountered every day because I needed to help them undo that thinking that it didn't apply." For instance, she would take the students to the parking lot and watch cars go by.

Ideas from the #MTBoS

Tina Cardone's Nix the Tricks

In 2013, Tina Cardone started a conversation about the various tricks students learn to get through math without really understanding it. Everyone seemed to have a pet peeve to share. This spurred a collaborative wiki, where educators contributed examples of tricks, along with alternative language that emphasized meaning. Some examples of tricks include turtle multiplication, "add a zero" (for multiplying by ten), "hungry" inequality signs, and FOIL. When students learn tricks without understanding, they misapply them. Then they make mistakes for which they have no intuition, making them unremarkable. As Tina writes about FOIL:

> *FOIL only applies to multiplying two binomials, a very specific task. There are other ways to multiply binomials that come from simpler distribution problems and are transferrable to later work such as multiplying larger polynomials and factoring by grouping. It also implies an order—a few of my honors precalculus students were shocked to learn that OLIF works just as well as FOIL does. Replace FOIL with the distributive property. It can be taught as soon as distribution is introduced. Students can start by distributing one binomial to each part of the other binomial. Then distribution is repeated on each monomial being multiplied by a binomial. As students repeat the procedure they will realize that each term in the first polynomial must be multiplied by each term in the second polynomial. This pattern, which you might term "each by each," carries through the more advanced versions of this exercise.*

Tina has since published *Nix the Tricks* (2013) to help other math teachers identify and avoid unproductive shortcuts.

To investigate rate, they would then predict how many cars go by in an hour. In a lesson on surface area, her students built three-dimensional objects out of blocks and then had to predict how much wrapping paper it would take to cover their structures. She carefully observed her students, found out their likes and dislikes, and she "breathed their interest into" the math curriculum. By showing students the mathematics around them, she helped them connect these ideas to their everyday lives.

Fawn similarly took advantage of students' environments to pose mathematics problems. One day, when supervising recess, she noticed that the four square court had been enlarged. "Hey," she shouted to her students, "when did they make this larger? I wonder what percent increase it is. What do you think?" Children shouted out estimates, marveling, "I love that you're asking us math questions at recess time." She used her prep to measure the old and new courts' dimensions, telling the story to her sixth-grade class and letting students go outside for five minutes to gather whatever information they needed to make an estimate. As a follow-up, her class generated a list of questions they could investigate through mathematics. (See Nguyen 2014 for more on this experience.) Both teachers support students' meaning making by connecting mathematics to students' worlds.

Meaningfulness Audit

1. What kind of participation gets rewarded in your math class? Does it reflect *learning* or *schooling* more?

2. How do you get students to cooperate without emphasizing compliance so much that it kills curiosity?

3. How do you help students develop student skills *while* supporting their learning? How do you grow the curiosity of good students who do not want to think too hard?

4. What opportunities do students have to introduce their own ideas in class? Pursue their own problems? How might you increase opportunities for students to introduce their ideas and pursue their own problems?

5 | Competence

Students quickly receive the message that they can only be smart when they are not who they are.

—CHRISTOPHER EMDIN, *FOR WHITE FOLKS WHO TEACH IN THE HOOD . . . AND THE REST OF Y'ALL TOO: REALITY PEDAGOGY AND URBAN EDUCATION*

In mathematics the art of asking questions is more valuable than solving problems.

—GEORG CANTOR, *DE AEQUATIONIBUS SECUNDI GRADUS INDETERMINATIS*

> What Competence Means

For better or worse, in our culture, mathematical success stands as the ultimate sign of smartness. In television and movies, writers often signal a character's innate intelligence by making him or her good at math. The downside of this is evident to those of us whose work involves math. In my two decades as a math educator, I have regularly encountered highly accomplished adults who confess, often with a sense of secret shame, that they were "never good at math." Of course, others declare this defiantly, as if to say that their success despite this weakness *proves* that mathematics is completely useless. Whether the confession comes with an air of regret or rebellion, these people are addressing the assumption that they are not as smart because of their struggles in math.

In short, there is a widespread perception that being good at math *equals* being smart in some global sense, and being "bad" at math means that a person is not as smart as people presume. As a thought experiment, I often ask my undergraduate students, all of whom are math majors, how their experiences in the world would be different if we ranked people's general smartness along another type of competency—say, musical virtuosity or mechanical skill. In other words, equating mathematical smartness with overall smartness is culturally specific, and it does not necessarily speak to a greater truth about human intelligence.

Just as our society values mathematical smartness more than other forms of smartness, so too do our classrooms. To understand how *competence* operates in mathematics classrooms, we need to come to grips with the cultural power of mathematical smartness. A motivational classroom needs to address students' competence directly, with sensitivity to the messages that students receive both in prior classes and in the broader culture. By reframing mathematical smartness while providing students opportunities to make and meet learning goals and experience success on optimally challenging activities, teachers can foster mathematical competence.

Issues of competence are highly affective, as they play on students' feelings of mastery in the subject, a key part of staying motivated. Students' affect in math class is critical to their decisions about staying with or abandoning a task or topic that presents a challenge. Longer-term, liking mathematics is a great predictor of staying with it over the course of their education.

Students' sense of competence is related to their sense of *self-efficacy*, the belief that they can successfully organize and perform a particular task. Students with high self-efficacy are frequently good learners, because they can set learning goals, use effective strategies, and monitor their own understanding and progress. Students with high self-efficacy are more likely to persist in learning challenging topics or working through difficult problems. Although self-efficacy is often thought of as an individual trait, we build our classrooms as environments where students have differing opportunities to experience it. As a general rule, how success gets defined in a classroom is therefore highly consequential to the development of a sense of mathematical competence. Additionally, these definitions of success align more or less with students' social identities. The particular funds of knowledge students bring from their homes and communities provide different kinds of strengths for them to bring into the classroom (Moll, Amanti, Neff, and Gonzalez 1992). When notions of success are at odds with students' culture, as Christopher Emdin's quote in the epigraph suggests, it creates impossible tensions for learners.

> **Competence:** *The need to be successful in meeting goals and in interacting with the environment.*

> Why Competence Matters

The cultural power of mathematical smartness makes math class a minefield of social risk. For example, students often fear that any visible signs of struggle not only implicate their precarious understanding of the topic at hand but also compromise their general sense of competence. In this way, a single mistake can be (wrongly) interpreted as a sign of general intellectual weakness. The high stakes attached to mistakes bring together the psychological and social dimensions of competence: in the cost-benefit analysis of social risk, nothing seems more costly than a highly public error and the resulting judgment from one's teachers and peers. This preoccupation with mistakes alone can impede students from participating in math class.

On the flip side, mathematics' cultural power gives math teachers an opportunity to have a tremendous positive impact on students. When teachers instill students with a sense of mathematical competence, they often, in turn, support greater overall academic confidence. If, for instance, math becomes a favorite subject, students attach themselves to its cultural power: when they share their love of math with important people in their lives, these folks will often express that they are impressed. More generally, students' sense of competence is central to their *mathematical identities*—how they and others see themselves as math learners—and therefore stands to make an impact on their future learning.

When teachers positively influence students' sense of mathematical competence, they support them in developing the self-efficacy beliefs that help them productively face learning challenges. Because mathematical competence is linked to perceptions of overall intellectual competence, when teachers cultivate it, they also support students' broader academic identities.

How Reframing Competence Shifts Social Risk

Schooling favors one type of mathematical competence: quick and accurate calculation. Given the ubiquity of work production classes in U.S. schools, with their emphasis on curricular coverage and student work output (see Chapter 4), it is understandable why this particular mathematical competence has risen above others as a sign of mathematical ability. However, looking at the history of mathematics as a field, it is clear that other types of competencies have been key to the development of new ideas and discoveries. Mathematician and explorer of infinite sets, Georg Cantor (1867), referred to one critical mathematical competence in the epigraph at the start of this chapter: asking good questions. New and important discoveries—ideas spanning from network theory to complex number spaces to topology—come out of good "what if" questions. Other competencies that have built the field of mathematics include:

- making astute connections

- seeing and describing patterns

- developing clear representations

- being systematic

- extending ideas.

A key point here is that *school mathematics typically reflects a small fragment of mathematical activity.* This is an enormous opportunity. Teachers can authentically incorporate richer types of disciplinary activities and reward broader mathematical competencies in their classrooms. In turn, by developing mathematical environments that engage a range of competencies, teachers reduce social risk, because the risk of participating does not hinge on one narrow way of being mathematically smart. In fact, more students benefit by experiencing the positive feelings of contributing their unique strengths and talents to the class' collective sense making.

❯ What Gets in the Way of Students' Sense of Competence

Two common instructional practices hinder students' sense of competence. First, work production mathematics classrooms emphasize finding correct answers to problems at hand. This results in competitiveness among high-achieving students and anxiety or apathy among low-achieving students. Work production classrooms place disproportionate value on quick and accurate calculation over other forms of competence, impeding many students from connecting their own interests and intellectual strengths to the content.

In emphasizing finding correct answers, teachers often engage in a second problematic practice: responding to student errors with quick correction instead of reflection. That is, they seek out the correct answer in order to move on with the lesson instead of using a mistake as a learning opportunity. This practice reinforces the problematic idea that some students "get it" and others do not. We see this in the following exchange, excerpted from a U.S. math classroom video collected for the Third International Mathematics and Science Study (n.d.):

Teacher: What's the complement of an angle of seven degrees? Ho?

Ho: Eighty-three.

Teacher: Eighty-three. The complement of eighty-four, Lindsey . . .

Lindsey: Sixteen.

Teacher: You sure about your arithmetic on that one?

Lindsey: Six?

Teacher: Six. Six degrees.

Ho's contribution to the class was more "successful" than Lindsey's because he provided the correct answer. When Lindsey answered incorrectly, the teacher's response was to prompt for quick correction, without even a perfunctory reminder of the meaning of *complementary*, a pointer to the diagram, or how to check one's mental math—teacher moves that would have emphasized conceptual understanding over accurate calculation. He cues her to recalculate, and the questioning intonation of her second response ("Six?") suggests that she is looking to him—not herself—as the mathematical authority.

Status in the Math Classroom

Over time, these common instructional practices result in noticeable status differences among students in math class. *Status* is the perception of students' academic capability and social desirability. Status is a useful, if somewhat complex, idea, but it is crucial to supporting students' sense of mathematical competence. Status describes widely held perceptions of who students are and what they have to offer. These perceptions are frequently derived from tracking systems that endow children with differential academic status by labeling some of them "honors students" while labeling others as "regular students." These perceptions are rooted in academic and social histories in prior mathematics classes, many of which likely valued narrow forms of mathematical competence. Status threats are probably the single greatest social risk posed by participation in mathematics class.

Because narrow competencies are valued in typical mathematics classrooms, students' prior academic histories get conflated with their abilities. That is, as students who respond quickly and accurately get repeatedly rewarded, they are widely perceived as "smart." As a result, other students look to them and defer to them in classroom discussions. On the other side, students who visibly struggle with quick and accurate calculation—or perhaps avoid trying to succeed because they do not care for the competition this mathematical competency often invites—are often perceived as less smart or even "dumb." As a result, their ideas are marginalized or ignored in classroom discussions. Judgments about academic status are often conflated with stereotypes about race, class, language, and gender. If students identify with (or are identified by) a stigmatized social group, they may experience the threat of these stereotypes and be hesitant to confirm people's low expectations of them (Steele and Aronson 1995).

Students' status is multidimensional: it is social as well as academic. For instance, students with low academic status but high social status may find ways to participate in class discussions, taking advantage of their peers' general interest in talking to them, even if they are not perceived to be "smart." Understanding participation patterns in terms of status dynamics opens up many possibilities for teacher action.

Status links competence to both belongingness and meaningfulness. When students' authentic mathematical competencies are recognized, this increases their academic status. This, in turn, reinforces their place in the classroom—their belongingness—because they have socially recognized, mathematically valuable contributions to make. Like everyone, students prefer to spend time in places where their strengths are valued. Incorporating students' intellectual competencies in a classroom gives them a profound sense of belonging and opens up new avenues for meaningfulness. If students' competencies have a place in the classroom, there are greater possibilities to connect students' curiosity to their mathematical learning.

❭ Strategies for Supporting Students' Sense of Mathematical Competence

The featured teachers' strategies for supporting students' sense of mathematical competence center on three related goals. First, they teach students *how* to learn by valuing different perspectives and challenges as important parts of learning. Second, they provide rich mathematical environments, along with structures that allow for exploration and making sense of ideas. Finally, they stay mindful of status threats and design their classroom routines to minimize them.

Valuing Different Perspectives and Challenges in Learning

If teachers value different forms of mathematical competence, then they relish the chance to hear different ways of thinking about ideas. As students share their thinking, they are likely to share emergent ideas that include mistakes. As a part of inviting students' different ways of thinking into their classrooms, the featured teachers worked with mistakes as learning opportunities. In addition to many other sense-making benefits, the chance to reflect on mistakes fosters students' sense of competence. It immediately engages other mathematical competencies, like asking good questions and making connections. Despite the differences in their contexts and approaches, all six teachers were clear about the importance of valuing different perspectives and normalizing mistakes in learning. This decreased the social risk of making mistakes, as they were not a direct threat to students' academic status, but instead a central part of the learning process. The teachers communicated this to their students in different ways.

Rafranz Davis, Sadie Estrella, and Fawn Nguyen invited different mathematical perspectives into their classrooms by letting their students know that they, as teachers, were also always learning. Rafranz's students knew that she was always curious about and making sense of their thinking: while her students were learning mathematics, she was learning about how they think about mathematics. When students would come up with a new perspective or make a new connection, she would thank them enthusiastically. "It's always 'Thank you so much!' It's a culture of constantly telling them thank you, thank you, thank you! Because I mean it. I mean that, you know, I'm learning so much and they're all learning." By positioning herself as a learner of their mathematical understanding, Rafranz not only modeled an enthusiasm for and delight in their sense making, she celebrated mathematical competencies like asking good questions, seeing and describing patterns, developing clear representations, being systematic, and extending ideas. All of these are fundamental to mathematical reasoning.

Sadie describes herself as a "lifelong learner." She constantly tries new and challenging things, whether it is hula dancing or sewing. These activities help her maintain her empathy for her students' experiences learning something that may be outside of their comfort zones. "When I was engaging in hula, I was so bad but I loved it to death. I realized this is what kids feel like in my classroom. This is what learning feels like. And I constantly need that memory." She uses these experiences when she is both planning and teaching lessons to help her students through the tough spots, keenly aware of the vulnerability learners can feel when they struggle. She reassures them: "I use the analogy of riding a bike. I [tell them], 'I'm not going to let you crash and burn. I will sometimes be beside you or sometimes I will be away from you, but I am not going to let you crash and burn.'"

Ideas from the #MTBoS

Andrew Gael: Advocating for Special Education Students in Math

When we look at the U.S. teacher labor market, two areas of frequent shortage are mathematics teachers and special education teachers. Andrew Gael is therefore a very rare bird, with specialties in both. Andrew illuminates the connections across these areas in his writing and advocacy. I always learn from reading his posts about what it means to support all the learners in our mathematics classrooms.

In a March 2016 post, he wrote:

> *The diversity of the classroom is at the epicenter of the learning environment. Diversity, however, can come to mean a variety of things.*
>
> *Recently, I have been reading about the concept of* neurodiversity. *Essentially, neurodiversity is based on the idea that brain diversity is similar to cultural diversity and the diversity of ecosystems.*
>
>> *We don't pathologize a calla lily by saying that it has a "petal deficit disorder." We simply appreciate its unique beauty . . . Similarly, we ought not to pathologize children who have different kinds of brains and different ways of thinking and learning. (Armstrong 2012)*
>
> *In his book* Neurodiversity in the Classroom, *Thomas Armstrong (2012) argues that the idea of neurodiversity is a "concept whose time has come." What he means by this is to reimagine how special education is constructed in our education system. The idea Armstrong highlights in his book is called "positive niche construction."*
>
> *Positive niche construction means developing hospitable climates for the diverse students who inhabit our classrooms. Recognizing and valuing multiple forms of competence is key to this work.*

Elsewhere, Andrew shared a great resource from the Educational Development Center on adaptations and modifications for various learning differences in math class (Brodesky et al. 2002).

Fawn invites her students' ideas by modeling her love of challenges with her students. She gives her students problems that she cannot solve right away. "Very honestly, I said, 'Guys, if you can solve this problem right away, well, I was stuck on these and I hope you feel that it's OK to be stuck because that was the first time I loved math.'" By bringing her unsolved problems to her students, Fawn sends several important messages about mathematical competence. First, she models that not knowing is a positive place to be with a problem. Second, she conveys her confidence in their smartness by seeking their help on problems she is interested in. Finally, while authentically solving problems alongside her students, she has an opportunity to share problem-solving competence by modeling her own thinking and strategies. Using herself as an example, she sends a clear and powerful message that being good at math is more than knowing answers.

Rich Mathematical Environments

All six featured teachers brought rich and authentic mathematics into their classrooms. They also all used mathematical tasks that share two important features:

1. They provide easy entry into mathematical situations.

2. Solutions require students to mathematically interpret those situations.

This type of low floor/high ceiling task, described in Chapter 4, is central to many of the different structures the featured teachers use. The following table gives some examples of different types of tasks that meet these criteria.

Structure	Description	Example
Challenges	Ask students to meet a set of conditions or create a counterexample.	Can you make a triangle from side lengths 6, 6, 10?
Analyzing Student Work	After students work a problem, they look at examples of student work to decide which methods are correct or what students' errors show about their understanding.	A jacket costs $32 originally. How much does it cost with a 25% discount? [Student work shows different methods and common errors.]
Estimation	To develop number sense, students make a quantitative prediction about something in the world.	How many cookies are eaten in this school at lunchtime?
Which One Doesn't Belong?	Students analyze a collection of pictures, graphs, or numbers and justify which one doesn't belong.	9 6 / 25 13

Structure	Description	Example
Would You Rather . . . ?	Students choose between two options and justify their answers mathematically.	Would you rather have a $9 \times 6 \times 3$-foot pool or a $5 \times 5 \times 4$-foot pool?
What If . . . ?	Students explore what happens if the conditions change. Great for extensions.	What would happen if we drew a series of n-gons as $n \to \infty$?
Opinions	Students compare strategies or approaches.	Which method is best for solving this system of equations? Why?
Always/ Sometimes/Never	Given a true-or-false type statement, students determine if it is always, sometimes, or never true.	Square numbers are even.
Why Do We Do That?	Students discuss the reasons behind familiar procedures.	Why do we rationalize the denominator?
Special Cases	Special cases help students build connections between ideas.	Why is $x^0 = 1$?

Some low floor/high ceiling question types. (Adapted from Stafford 2016.)

Chris Luzniak's debate questions use these kinds of tasks to enable students to use and share varied competencies. As he explained, "My questions are purposely low-stake, something where anyone can have an opinion: 'What's the best mistake you see?' 'What's the best way to start this problem?' There's something that everyone can grasp onto." All of the question types in the table can be adapted to a debate format, providing students with the opportunity to make sense of their mathematical ideas. Some examples of topics Chris' students have debated are:

Every number has a square root.
The best way to solve $x^2 + 3x - 18$ is by completing the square.

The first question has an always/sometimes/never structure. As students debate, they have to make important distinctions between numbers that are perfect squares and have whole number roots and those that do not. This engages the mathematical competencies of making astute connections and seeing and describing patterns. As they explore further, they come up against negative numbers and, depending on where they are in their learning, they may wonder about or see the need for imaginary numbers. These considerations involve the competencies of being systematic by exhausting different types of numbers and extending ideas.

The second question is a best-method opinion prompt. As students discuss whether or not completing the square is the best method, they need to consider and describe alternative methods. This has tremendous metacognitive benefits, demanding that students explain their reasons for choosing one approach over another. As they do, they have a chance to describe patterns they look for in quadratics that inform these judgments. All of these debates provide ample opportunities for students to ask each other good questions and make connections.

Similarly, many of Elizabeth Statmore's Talking Points use low floor/high ceiling prompts to supports students' exploratory talk, with this structure especially supporting students' comparison of their interpretations. As Elizabeth explained, "Interpretations and strategies [for solving problems] often differ. They require slower thinking to share with a class. A lot of mathematics can be drawn out by comparing them, which moves away from the 'one right answer' mentality." Recall from Chapter 2 that the Talking Points structure asks students to review a list of statements and take a justified position on them, deciding whether they agree, disagree, or are unsure about the statement. Many of Elizabeth's Talking Points statements use the formats in the earlier table, but as declarations instead of questions.

For example, here are two Talking Points statements about geometry:

Pentagons have fewer right angles than rectangles.
Quadrilaterals tessellate.

Both of these prompts have an always/sometimes/never format. The Talking Points structure requires more than an answer, though: it asks students to think about why they think what they do. As students explore their thinking about whether they agree, disagree, or are unsure, some will inevitably start sketching, seeing if they can draw pentagons with four right angles (developing clear representations) or if they can find a nontessellating quadrilateral (being systematic). The pentagon question invites numerical analysis as well, as students can consider the sum of its interior angles as a way of imagining the counterexample to the statement (making astute connections). The discourse structures of Math Debate and Talking Points support students' mathematical explorations and value broader types of mathematical competencies.

Staying Mindful of Status Threats

Normalizing uncertainty is really important in Peg Cagle's classroom, where many gifted students experience impostor syndrome: being wrong might suggest that they do not really belong. The status threat of mistakes can implicate their whole identity as students. As described earlier, many students experience the status-threat tied to their racial, linguistic, and gendered identities known as *stereotype threats* (Steele and Aronson 1995): the anxiety that one slip may confirm others' preconceptions of who they are and their abilities. One way Peg invited her students to slow down and think was to emphasize the competence of asking good questions. She had a poster on the wall that said, "Ask, don't tell." As she explained, "When you ask a good question, everybody starts thinking. When you answer it, almost everybody stops. So put as much time and thought into forming questions as forming answers." During discussions, if students did not have an answer to a question, they were constantly encouraged to formulate a question about it.

As Peg's example illustrates, the particular needs of students, along with their histories in math and school, shape how we cultivate and preserve their sense of competence. When I taught in working- and middle-class high schools, I had to build my students' confidence that they could do challenging work. Many of them did not believe they were mathematically smart, so it became my task to help them recognize their own competencies so they could persevere with difficult problems. In contrast, Peg had to reassure her students that they could struggle and still be "smart." We both attended to students' sense of competence, but we had different paths as teachers to meet the needs of our particular students.

Competence Audit

1. What kinds of competencies are valued in your classroom? Where do students have a chance to show them?

2. Consider the last few activities you have done in your class. Did they provide multiple entry points toward a rich mathematical idea? If not, can you use the table in this chapter to adapt them to become low ceiling/high floor questions?

3. When you look at your class roster, can you identify at least one way that every student is mathematically smart?

4. When you think of students who struggle, do they have competencies that you might better support by redesigning some of your class activities?

5. When you think of students who have a history of high achievement, do they value other ways to be smart aside from quick and accurate calculation? Do they value other competencies in themselves? In others?

6 | Accountability

The teacher's job is not to transmit knowledge, nor to facilitate learning. It is to engineer effective learning environments for the students. The key features of effective learning environments are that they create student engagement and allow teachers, learners, and their peers to ensure that the learning is proceeding in the intended direction. The only way we can do this is through assessment. That is why assessment is, indeed, the bridge between teaching and learning.

—DYLAN WILIAM, *EMBEDDED FORMATIVE ASSESSMENT*

Teaching is listening. Learning is talking.

—DEBORAH MEIER, *THE POWER OF THEIR IDEAS: LESSONS FOR AMERICA FROM A SMALL SCHOOL IN HARLEM*

> **What Accountability Means**

In Chapter 4, I described the ways schooling can interfere with meaningful learning. Students can play the game of school by sitting quietly, producing work, and earning grades without much understanding, which is a hallmark of deeper learning. Conversely, they can learn a lot of content but fail to produce the work that gets their learning certified. Equally worrisome, they might behave in ways that get them excluded from the classroom, putting up more barriers to showing (and growing) what they know. Some students' inability to "do school" precludes them from having their learning institutionally acknowledged.

Accountability and Assessment

These tensions come out in classroom accountability systems, particularly when it comes to grading and feedback. If our classrooms are, as sociologist Dan Lortie (1975) described, self-contained cells, grades are windows that give others a glimpse at what happens inside. These windows open in a number of ways. Increasingly, schools use online grade books accessible to parents and guardians. Administrators often look at passing rates in math classes at the end of terms. Parents, future teachers, and postsecondary institutions may only ever see a letter grade as a summary of students' learning. Indeed, schooling is built on credit accrual, which, in turn, depends on grading.

Ideally, we should have clear, consistent, and fair systems to give students credit for their work. Yet all kinds of complexity immediately arise: the students who learn but do not produce scorable work; students who turn in work but do not learn much; students who struggle on tests but demonstrate their learning in other ways that are not weighted into the grading system. This aspect of accountability is called *assessment*. Assessment describes how teachers gather evidence about what a student knows and understands about mathematics and then makes inferences about that evidence.

> **Assessment:** *The processes teachers use to gather evidence and make inferences about what students know and understand.*

Beyond Assessment: Classroom Norms for Accountability

Classroom accountability systems extend beyond assessment and grading. *Accountability* literally refers to responsibility and obligation, so it also refers to acceptable ways to act in class. These are best described as *classroom norms*. Norms shape how learning transpir‹ a classroom, so teachers need to consider how they are established and maintained.

> **Classroom norms:** *Agreed-upon ways of behaving in the classroom.*

Norms can not only shape how learning happens, but they also provide standards for discourse. In their studies of collaborative learning, educational researchers Elizabeth Cohen and Rachel Lotan (2014) have written extensively about teaching methods that make students accountable to each other to support productive engagement. One component of their approach centers on fostering norms of student interdependence, helping children find ways to value each other's strengths and learn together. A good illustration of this aspect of classroom accountability is found in the Institute for Learning (IFL) at the University of Pittsburgh's tools for Accountable Talk (see Institute for Learning 2015). These tools provide classroom discourse strategies that hold students accountable in three ways: accountable to the classroom learning community; accountable to accurate knowledge; and accountable to rigorous thinking.

Elaborating on these ideas for science and math classrooms, educational researchers Randi Engle and Faith Conant (2002) describe how students' ideas need to be held up to disciplinary norms, as well as those established by the classroom community. As one example, mathematicians have disciplinary norms about what counts as justification. For instance, in making mathematical claims, we need to identify the cases for which a statement is true. Noticing a few cases of a pattern does not support a general claim. A claim such as "All numbers have square roots" would be understood differently depending on whether we are looking at the set $\{1, 4, 9, 16, \ldots\}$, the real number line, or the complex numbers. Similarly, the truth of the claim that "parallel lines never meet" depends on whether we are drawing those lines on a plane or a sphere. Disciplinary norms of mathematics require us to specify the scope of our claim under particular conditions. Whether those conditions need to be explicit or taken for granted changes depending on the context. (For instance, if we are teaching Euclidean geometry, the spherical case may not be relevant, so it may not need to be specified.) This, in turn, changes what counts as justification and when it may be seen as adequate. Disciplinary norms for justification can be incorporated into classroom discussions, giving students greater access to the content while holding them accountable to certain standards. Importantly, these disciplinary norms often invite the multiple mathematical competencies described in Chapter 5. (For a great discussion of mathematical argumentation, see Lakatos 2015.)

Classroom norms can mitigate some of the tensions between schooling and learning. For instance, treating mistakes as learning opportunities can be made into a classroom norm. This norm pushes against widely held assumptions that equate being a good student with being smart. But not all tensions can be so readily recognized—or remedied. For teachers striving for motivational math classrooms, it is worth doing an audit to see where assessment practices contradict classroom norms. For instance, I have seen teachers try to establish norms like "Everyone's ideas are important" and carry this out by inviting and valuing multiple mathematical competencies during classwork. They subsequently undermine this message by relying solely on assessments that value one competence—the usual quick and accurate calculation that permeates school math. To have a coherent classroom accountability system, what we value in our assessments needs to reflect what we value in our classroom norms. We stand to lose students' trust if we say one thing and then do another, especially because assessments often "count" more: they have a public face and a longer future, as the resulting grades travel with students as they move through school.

How Classroom Accountability Systems Can Shift Social Risk

When done thoughtfully, social risk can be reduced through both the assessment and norm components of classroom accountability systems. Undoubtedly, assessments often pose tremendous social risks: this is the root of much test anxiety. In both the formative assessments where teachers check for understanding and the summative ones where they evaluate learning, students' sense of competence is made vulnerable to external judgment, threatening their status—and perhaps even their sense of belongingness—in the classroom. Researchers who study productive classroom assessment practices talk about the importance of designing systems that emphasize *assessment for learning*. Both during and after instruction, teachers gather evidence of what students know and understand. They then use that evidence to inform subsequent instruction and to guide students' future learning.

This second part is key: assessment for learning provides feedback to support students. At the same time, feedback is tricky because students do not always experience it as supportive. As educational psychologist Susan Nolen (2011) describes:

> *Similar feedback might have different effects on student engagement, depending on the relationships between student and teacher, among peers, and between students and parents. Telling a student that they have tried hard might be perceived as praise for compliance by one child, as an indicator of low ability by another, or as encouragement to keep working by a third, depending on the student's goals, the importance or meaning of the task in the social context, and the kinds of feedback given at other times or to other children. (321)*

In other words, the way students understand teachers' feedback is highly contextual, shaped by classroom norms and relationships, as well as alignments between what the teacher means and what students actually hear. For this reason, home culture can also play a huge role in how students experience feedback, because some cultures normalize direct critique, making feedback more natural and welcome. In other cultures, the same direct critique can be seen as being rude or unkind, a rejecting experience that threatens students' sense of belonging. This points us back to the centrality of trust and belongingness, discussed in Chapter 3. In the best situations, teachers communicate explicitly that their goal in giving feedback is to both inform their instruction and guide students' learning, teaching their students their purpose and addressing potential misunderstandings.

In a lot of classrooms, norms of competition and comparison prevail and are fraught with social risk. Students are viewed as smart for answering quickly and correctly, so they vie to be the fastest. Although this is especially true in classes filled with academically high-status students—like honors or accelerated sections—it is not limited to these settings. When teachers deliberately work toward norms around multiple math smartnesses ("Everybody has something to contribute") and reduce the concern over inaccuracies ("Mistakes are learning opportunities"), it shifts the cost-benefit analysis of participation. Student ideas are explicitly invited, and errors are not an indictment of anybody's competence.

What Gets in the Way of Accountability

Both the assessment and norm components of classroom accountability systems can be distorted by common schooling practices. Two of the many ways that assessment can be distorted include relying on overly narrow evidence and using what I call an *isomorphic pretest*.

Classroom assessment systems often rely on overly narrow evidence to ascertain what a student has learned by only counting paper-and-pencil tests. Although some students can reliably demonstrate their understanding there, other students can better show their learning in other ways, such as untimed tasks or projects. School is not typically organized to support teachers in using and grading open-ended activities, because they require significantly more time to assess than right-or-wrong answers on a test. This skews many classroom assessment systems to validate some kinds of learning and understanding over others.

Second, the common teaching practice of giving an isomorphic pretest or a study guide, one that has the same problems but different numbers, distorts the resulting grades. Isomorphic pretests favor students who know how to play school by giving them a chance to learn and reproduce patterns without deep understanding, while disadvantaging students ho are less school savvy. These pretests can also provide a defensive cover for teachers who e not managing to support deeper learning in their classrooms: they can show a group of "successful" students who managed to "learn" the material, as evidenced by their pattern reproduction, making a case for adequate instruction. "If these kids can get it," the message goes, "it can't be the teaching. It must be something wrong with the kids who can't get it." In an otherwise unmonitored classroom, this logic can go far, to the detriment of both school-savvy and less school-savvy students' learning.

Many commonplace norms can also distort classroom accountability. Aside from the widespread "competition" norm, tacitly achieved treaties govern many classrooms (Powell, Farrar, and Cohen 1985). That is, students trade in their compliance and cooperation—student behaviors that alleviate the challenges of crowded classrooms—for minimal demands for engagement by the teacher. When I have worked with teachers trying out open-ended tasks for the first time, I will often hear of "pushback" or "resistance" from the students. These student responses indicate that teachers are violating their part of the treaty by going beyond minimal demands for engagement and increasing intellectual press. Put differently, by using open-ended tasks, teachers raise the social risk, leaving students open to judgment because they cannot rely on the usual rituals of math class. Treaties may, as their name suggests, keep the peace, but they reflect norms of minimal engagement that interfere with deeper learning.

> Strategies for Creating Coherent and Respectful Classroom Accountability Systems

Classroom accountability systems encompass a lot of teaching practice. My goal here is not to review all aspects of an ideal system—there are other resources for that, notably *Mathematics Assessment* (Stenmark 1991), the Shell Centre's Formative Assessment Lessons (n.d.), the previously mentioned IFL Accountable Talk tools, and Dylan Wiliam and Siobhán Leahy's *Embedding Formative Assessment* (2015). Instead, I hope to highlight how the organization of accountability can contribute to a motivational classroom and point to strategies the featured teachers have employed to mitigate social risk. The teachers work to create coherent and respectful accountability systems that communicate two central norms: everybody is here to learn, and everyone is capable. To do this, they work deliberately to renegotiate the classroom treaty through structures and strategic feedback to individual students on their participation.

Renegotiating the classroom treaty requires a clear vision for what student participation can look like, structures to support that vision, along with the determination to see it through. The featured teachers all work toward classroom accountability systems whe.. open, respectful communication can take place. Before this work can begin, teachers need to establish a foundation of trust. "Student accountability begins and ends with trust," Rafranz Davis tells me. "Part of our trust system is in understanding that feedback is a part of growth. We all give and receive feedback, and understanding that helps protect the sanctity of the system."

All of the teachers have many students who have not been in math classrooms structured around sense making and two-way dialogue. They assume that they will need to renegotiate the classroom treaty, establishing that foundation of trust. All of the featured teachers are clear on this point: students' passive compliance will no longer be exchanged for minimal academic press. Instead, the teachers expect active learning and let students know the rules of the game: everyone participates, listening matters, and we focus on ideas.

Everyone Participates

In my own observations, I see teachers struggle to move students past their initial reluctance to participate and make it clear that active involvement is required. The same structures that the teachers use to shift notions of competence also provide tools for accountability. (See Chapters 2 and 5 for more on these.) Sadie Estrella's Counting Circles, Fawn Nguyen's Visual Patterns, Elizabeth Statmore's Talking Points, and Chris Luzniak's Math Debates all support the expectation that everybody participates in class.

Setting Expectations from the Start

All of the teachers emphasize how critical the first days are for setting these expectations for their students, particularly because their expectations may differ from what students are used to in math class. "It's entirely intentional that I begin setting norms and structures on the first day of school," Fawn explains. She introduces the Visual Pattern and Mental Math routines from the start. By launching the new school year *showing* students what it means to do math in her class, Fawn renegotiates the classroom treaty through these new norms and structures. She says, "I need to provide students with ample opportunities to experience the culture that we have set up. We need to establish and maintain a culture that's safe for sharing and discussing mathematics, safe for making mistakes, and a culture that honors each person's right to contribute. There needs to be a firm belief among everyone that mathematics is a vital social endeavor. Building this culture takes time."

At the beginning of the year, Sadie starts her students with ten minutes of Counting Circles. She does not press students to talk beyond that at first, but she finds that "eventually, they feel so comfortable that during the main lesson they are talking again. You can't help but let it seep out." Giving students a chance to grow comfortable with the shifting expectations is also key, reducing social risk. Indeed, explicitly naming expectations with students has been identified as a crucial step as teachers move toward ambitious instruction (Selling 2016).

Normalizing Challenge

Peg Cagle, the architect, uses design thinking to help students learn new ways of participation. "I move the things that are in the way of sense making." As she explains it, Peg hones in on classroom habits that inhibit students' deeper mathematical thinking. The fear of being wrong and the fear of being confused are high on the list of obstacles, so many of her renegotiation strategies attend to those student concerns. For example, her high-achieving students sometimes try to read her expressions for cues about whether their thinking is right or wrong. She explicitly reworks this particular habit, and they soon learn, much to their chagrin, that she has an excellent poker face when she hears their ideas. This helps establish that, especially in the exploratory stage of her lessons, she is more interested in *what* their ideas are than in whether they are right or wrong.

She also normalizes the challenge of learning new mathematics. She asks students to help her make a list of what is hard about a topic. "It wasn't 'What are you confused about,' it was, 'What is hard about this topic'—whether it's connecting the ideas to things you already know, whether it's because it feels like it's a departure from things that we've done in the past, whether it's the notation, whether it's the particular application, what can you think of that's hard. We want to list everything that's hard on the board.' And very often I would tell them not to raise their hands, just shout them out, and I'd write as fast as I could, while they shouted out everything that's hard. They would say four things and I would step back and I'd go, 'Well I can think of at least five more things. Really, that's all you guys can think of?'" These discussions reduced students' distress, making their confusion an expected part of the learning process. In this framing, challenge does not become something unpleasant that needs to be avoided. Instead, as Peg says, she wants her students to see that "this is challenging, but that's what makes it fun and worthwhile."

Inviting Increased Participation

Peg uses small whiteboards to invite student participation. Something about the easily erasable surface gives students more confidence to participate and try out rough draft ideas. This design has been explored in great detail by mathematics education researcher Peter Liljedahl (2016). He has found that student groups are more eager to start solving problems and there is more discussion, participation, persistence, and nonlinearity when they work on whiteboards than on paper. He also notes that when the whiteboards are positioned vertically on the wall, this invites even more sustained positive engagement.

Some teachers modify well-known accountability strategies to reduce their social risk. For example, cold calling—when teachers ask a student a question without the student's indication that they want to contribute—is a common accountability strategy, communicating the expectation that everyone participates. Cold calling has rightly been criticized for increasing social risk by putting students on the spot, making them vulnerable to judgment. However, Chris Luzniak has developed a cold call routine that lowers its social risk. First, he usually gives students a minute or two to write answers. This think time means that all students have had some opportunity to reflect on his question. Also, he often asks for volunteers, so cold calling is not his only strategy. When he does cold call, he has found a way to make it playful. "I randomly pick on people using note cards with everyone's name on it. I call them the 'cards of destiny.'" The randomness of his routine is also important. A lot of cold call methods involve nonrandom selection of students, where the teacher looks for a child who is not paying attention. That form of cold call turns teachers' questions into a form of control rather than a genuine contribution to the class' inquiry. Additionally, although the humorous name may seem beside the point—a cold call is a cold call—it serves an important motivational function. Specifically, silliness helps lower social risk. If, for example, a teacher dramatizes the possible threat of being selected by a card of destiny, a student's potential stumble can be met with impish encouragement:

- "But, Amara, you must have something to say! This is your destiny!"
- "Can somebody help César fulfill his destiny?"

In making the cold call moment playful, Chris offsets the risk of not knowing through the benefits of participation. Instead of the worst outcome of a cold call being "caught" not knowing, the worst outcome becomes the teacher's friendly ribbing, with the possible support of other students' contributions.

Using Collaboration to Foster Accountability

Many of the featured teachers develop class norms that allow students to learn together. This also lowers social risk while keeping students accountable to one another. For example, Fawn's students often work in groups, and she has them lean on each other if one person does not know how to respond to her questions. "When students say they don't have anything to say, it doesn't mean I skip them. I tell them that they have two minutes: 'I want you to try and set up the problem like you would on paper and then talk them through it, did you estimate . . .?' Even if the student has nothing to say after two minutes, she has [her group] think through it with her." In Fawn's view, the two minutes of active thinking matter. It gets students on a path toward making a contribution in the future.

Encouraging Quiet Students to Participate

When figuring out how to respond to quiet students, the teachers try to understand the nature of students' limited participation. Not all quiet students are quiet for the same reasons. At times, quietness is rooted in temperament: some students are inclined to hang back until they feel confident about what is going on, but they are listening intently to everything in class. These students do not contribute frequently, but, when they do, their contributions add a lot to conversations. This kind of quiet is less of a concern and can even be acknowledged: "Raymond, I notice you don't talk a lot, but when you do, I always love hearing what you have to say." Sometimes, quietness comes from inattention. Because of the dialogue in the featured teachers' classrooms (as opposed to typical teacher-centered talk), students get brought back into the classroom flow, perhaps with the help of their peers, and confused students' ideas become a resource to uncover different ways of thinking about the topics at hand.

Other times, quietness signals students' lack of confidence. That is, students reveal some understanding in their work or small-group conversations, but they do not have the confidence to participate in whole-class conversations. With these students, the teachers seek out one-on-one check-ins. Chris calls these "doorway talks," and Peg calls them "sidebars." (When I note the different names, Peg tells me, "Trying to deal with calculators and rulers at the end of class, I couldn't make it to the doorway!") Chris offers supportive encouragement during doorway talks. "I might say to a kid, 'You know, you had really good ideas today, and I would have loved to have heard more of them in the conversation we had at the end. I think you have a lot more to contribute than you give yourself credit for.'" Sometimes, the teachers encourage good ideas to become public without directly addressing a student. Chris explains that he might say something like, "I haven't heard from this corner of the room." He then asks other students to hold their ideas while waiting for a contribution from the quiet group.

Sometimes students' reluctance to participate comes from a fear of having nothing to say. Of course, secondary students are adolescents, a developmental phase known for mischief and hijinks. Sometimes students "play" with the discourse structures. They know teachers are listening for certain phrases. They might use a phrase in an exaggerated way, a verbal wink to their peers. "Well, my *conjecture* is . . ." When that happens in Peg's classroom, she plays right back, with a nod to their acting skills. "Oscar-worthy!" she says, sweeping by their desks.

Ideas from the #MTBoS

Heather Kohn's Strategies
for Emergent Bilinguals

Heather Kohn earned a special certification in Sheltered Instruction for English Language Learners (also known as *emergent bilinguals*, to emphasize their linguistic competence). In Sheltered Instruction, content area teachers pay attention to developing language, providing scaffolds for reading and writing. Two strategies Heather has shared are:

Partner Reading for Comprehension
- Partner 1 reads aloud one word problem.
- Partner 1 questions or comments about the content, language, structure, or vocabulary from the problem.
- Partner 2 provides clarification or positive feedback.

Cut and Grow
- Students look at a student work sample that demonstrated some understanding but not mastery.
- They cut the question apart.
- They write additional text or diagrams to strengthen the response.

Both of these activities allow students to develop their second language competence while engaging in grade-level content, a goal of sheltered instruction. Additionally, instruction for emergent bilinguals includes paying attention to their gestures when they are offering explanations, including many visual examples, and having keen linguistic awareness. Especially important are: confusing synonyms (e.g., square *roots* vs. plant *roots;* a *table* of values vs. a dining *table*), which vary in different languages; false cognates in the English language (e.g., *figure* in English is not the same as *figura* in Spanish); and semantic complexity (e.g., "less than" sentences are more complex than "minus" in word problems). These linguistic features of our textbooks and word problems may keep students from showing what they know.

ᵧond temperament and lack of confidence, it can sometimes be difficult to ascertain ᵢny students are quiet. Some students are quiet due to language differences, in which case the teacher needs to modify instruction to give them more access to the ideas.

Rafranz draws reluctant students out by paying attention to what they care about and the interests they bring to the classroom. For instance, she might seamlessly move a conversation about an after-school job to questions of what their earning goals are, then to a calculation of how long it will take to meet them. Sadie sometimes asks students who do not like to talk in class to write summaries of what they learned to check their understanding. These practices illustrate how teachers can meet quiet students where they are, while monitoring their mathematical learning and possibly drawing them out. If you are really stuck, it might be helpful to check in with colleagues about the student's performance in prior years or in other subjects. If students are deeply disengaged across classes or if this is a new affect for them, this may signal a deeper issue that requires the help of a counselor.

The Challenge of Talkative Students

Talkative students pose another kind of challenge to the expectation that everyone participates. On the one hand, they can be wonderful models by sharing their thinking. They can be the reliably "brave volunteers" who explore their thinking publicly when the rest of the class sits stone-faced. Teachers can lean on them to break the ice and get conversations started. On the other hand, they can be domineering, making it difficult for other students to get a word in edgewise. The quiet students who need to think before they speak have their counterparts in talkative students who think *by* talking. Asking for their silence sometimes gets heard as asking them not to think. Rafranz, who identifies with the talkative students, worked with them on learning to ask good questions. In this way, they could continue to engage and talk, as they are inclined to do, but the other students would still have a chance to think and learn. When I had students like that in my own classes, I made sure to assure them that I valued their engagement but that I needed them to find other strategies for processing so that other students could be heard.

Sometimes, students with impaired executive functioning, like those with attention deficit hyperactivity disorder or who have experienced trauma, have a hard time with the turn-taking aspect of classroom dialogue, so not only do they talk a lot, they also struggle to take turns, interrupting others. Again, teachers can respond by valuing students' ideas while helping them participate more effectively: "I love your enthusiasm! But we need to take turns so that we can hear each other."

Finally, students who are highly confident in their understanding and want to explain to others may also be very talkative. Teachers need to judge the extent to which this behavior is altruistic, a sense of excitement about sharing knowledge, and the extent to which it shuts conversations down. (These, by the way, are not mutually exclusive.) In the first case, students can be coached toward asking questions of their classmates, channeling their impulse to talk into something constructive. In the second case, the dominance can be corrosive to the classroom environment, and the students might need stronger redirection, such as through sidebars or doorway talks or indirect address. ("Let's hear from somebody else.") If a student consistently struggles with impulse control despite careful coaching, it might be helpful to check in with other teachers about the behaviors they see and strategies they find effective.

Listening Matters

We typically think of classroom participation as the sum of students' spoken contributions. In the featured teachers' classrooms, listening is also an important form of participation. By making listening a central activity in their classes, the teachers support students in another critical and often less risky form of participation. In productive conversations, ideas build on one another, which requires attention to others' contributions.

When people first learn of discourse structures like Math Debates, Counting Circles, or Talking Points, they pay attention to how these invite students to speak. Equally important, however, is the ways that these structures invite student listening. Because they aim for dialogue, being a good listener is as important as being a good speaker. Elizabeth, through Talking Points, makes it very clear that good listening matters. "I try to explain to kids that your job, what you are going to be assessed on, is how well you are receiving what other people are saying when it's their turn to speak." In fact, when I asked Chris what a good math discussion looked like in his class, he named listening as a key indicator. "They're expressing their thinking out loud, and other kids are listening, saying, 'You know what? I thought like that too!'"

Listening, as a skill, not only builds classroom dialogue, it can help students become better learners. As Sadie describes, she knows she has achieved something important when her students learn to listen to themselves. "I always listen for them to catch themselves making a mistake as they are verbalizing," she tells me. "They're like, 'Oh wait! That doesn't make sense.'" Learning to listen does more than help them participate in the classroom discussion. It models the kind of self-monitoring—the metacognition—that makes students more effective learners.

The teachers use the discourse structures to develop norms for listening and dialogue, but they support other participation norms as well: turn taking, justifying reasoning, grounding opinions in specific examples, just to name a few. Even when the teachers are not using specific structures, their expectations about participation carry over into other classroom activities. Students need to both contribute and listen during all classroom activities.

Focusing on Ideas

Students are often inhibited from class participation because they dislike being evaluated: the possibility of judgment brings risk. Math class often feels particularly evaluative, because it is widely viewed as subject with right and wrong answers, making little room for opinion or interpretation. To focus on ideas, the purpose of teachers' questions needs to change. The featured teachers all let students know that they are interested in digging into their ideas, not on finding the correct answer. Instead of being a game of "gotcha" to punitively identify inattentive or confused students, the featured teachers' questions reflect a deep curiosity about students' thinking. "I very often frame things about me being curious," Peg explains. She checks in frequently with students about how they make sense of lessons. Not only does this invite them to share their thinking, but satisfying this genuine curiosity also provides her with feedback on what is and is not working instructionally. This is the heart of good formative assessment.

One way to shift the evaluative climate is to shift toward a climate of conjecturing. In Math Debates, for instance, students share ideas by saying their conjectures as "claims." In Talking Points, the *ideas* are the focal point to expand on by stating whether they agree, disagree, or are unsure. The very presence of this last option normalizes uncertainty about mathematical understanding.

Fawn emphasizes the importance of students giving and responding to critiques of their thinking. Sometimes, she models critiquing from the genuine confusion she experiences when students present in class and she does not understand their ideas. She can honestly express her questions, modeling questions like, "Why did you think that? Could you explain more?" Her questions are motivated by her curiosity. Eventually, the students learn to be curious about each other's thinking and ask each other similar questions. Her goal is to make them critical thinkers—and she lets them know that this is her purpose: "We are citizens. We have to be educated and we want to make wise decisions. When you just go along with other people, you're not going to learn anything."

Rafranz's curiosity about her students' thinking has helped her develop numerous strategies to uncover it, even when students cannot necessarily express themselves in the classroom's primary language. Rafranz's classes often had emergent bilingual students, usually fluent Spanish speakers who were learning English. She had them share their ideas through visual representations. At other times, her students made videos explaining their thinking in their native language. These recordings gave Rafranz an opportunity to

Ideas from the #MTBoS

Anna Blinstein's Formative Assessment Meetings

Anna uses regularly scheduled meetings to check in with students about the progress they are making in her class. She adapted this practice from Ron Ritchhart's *Creating Cultures of Thinking* (2015). Here is what she does:

1. She schedules twenty-minute biweekly meetings with each student. She has these meetings before school, during lunch, during free periods, tutorial, and after school.

2. She discusses work the student has turned in during the last two weeks. Anna goes through their work with them and gives verbal feedback. Either she or the student records a summary of the feedback.

3. She discusses the students' overall progress, how they are incorporating previous feedback, and asking for how they can be better supported.

This practice communicates caring, supports relatedness, and emphasizes students' competence. Anna reports that through these formative assessment meetings, she has been able to push her students toward more challenging problems because she helps them make sense of her feedback.

I used a similar conference structure in my work with the Seattle teachers. We held them less frequently, but the payoff in students' sense of care and the teachers' investment in their learning was tremendous. These conversations helped students engage teachers' feedback and adjust their participation accordingly.

rewatch and rewind. By finding ways to include the thinking of *all* her students, Rafranz communicated how central students' ideas were in her classroom.

Of course, we cannot entirely escape the evaluative nature of schooling. The featured teachers hope that the foundation of trust, focus on learning, and mutual support helps students navigate the potential social risk that come from assessment and grading. For Fawn, the relationships she develops with her students are key to making this work. "Because I treat my students with respect and kindness, I hope they know that the grades they earn in my class are solely related to their abilities to show mastery of the content and process standards."

Accountability Audit

1. Look through your roster. Can you identify students whose grades do not reflect their level of understanding? What contradictions might this point to in your classroom accountability system?

2. What are the various ways that you gather evidence about what students know?

3. How do you make inferences from these various pieces of evidence?

4. What are the various feedback systems for reflecting *how* students are learning in your classroom? These can be about their academic learning or for their productive participation.

5. How do you help students learn to take up feedback, both in class, on their work, and regarding their participation?

6. What norms can you identify in your classroom?

7. Are there gaps between what you say you value and what students do? If so, what structures or routines can you incorporate that might help you teach them new ways of being in math class?

7 | Autonomy

For me, the child is a veritable image of becoming, of possibility, poised to reach towards what is not yet, towards a growing that cannot be predetermined or prescribed. I see her and I fill the space with others like her, risking, straining, wanting to find out, to ask their own questions, to experience a world that is shared.

—MAXINE GREENE, COMMENCEMENT ADDRESS,
BANK STREET COLLEGE

What is the greatest sign of success for a teacher [. . .]? It is to be able to say, "The children are now working as if I did not exist."

—MARIA MONTESSORI, *THE ABSORBENT MIND*

> What Autonomy Means

Ms. Gudinoff decides to have her eighth-grade students work in pairs on the fraction task introduced in Chapter 1. She shows how to think about finding the fraction of the square represented by rectangle A. She checks in to make sure everybody understands, and they nod their assent. "OK," she says, "now work with your partner to find the names of the other fractions. Try to work together and only call me over if you are really stuck." Predictably, Mia and Riley dig into the task, eagerly discussing what fractions the different regions represent. Many students work quietly, side by side. A few pairs start arguing, even throwing in a few choice insults. Before long, Ms. Gudinoff finds herself pulled in too many directions: Should she answer Mia's math question, squelch the conflict brewing between Zachary and Tobias, or help Imen get started? If only there were six of her, maybe this would be doable.

In this vignette, Ms. Gudinoff is overwhelmed by her students' dependence on her. She wants to give them a chance to do what the mathematics education research literature says: let her students discuss rich problems so that they can learn the content deeply. She launches the lesson by working through an example, but when the students are sent to work independently, it does not go well. Students need her, for all kinds of different things, all across the room. They do not exhibit autonomy when doing mathematics.

Autonomy refers to the ability to make choices and act on one's free will. Sometimes, teachers respond to looming classroom chaos by making structures that primarily *control* students' behavior. They design management systems that focus primarily on coercing students into cooperative behavior through an assertion of their authority or even threats. Coercion, however, does not make students independent. As an alternative, teachers need to give students structures, strategies, and norms for interacting in ways that will support productive interactions that the teacher does not need to constantly oversee.

Scaffolding is a common word in education circles, a metaphor from construction. It refers to the structures we, as teachers, put in place to support students as they build their knowledge and understanding. Scaffolding differs from coercion, because students have opportunities to act autonomously within the structures in ways that support productive learning interactions. Additionally, just as construction scaffolding is meant to serve as a temporary support during a building's formation, so too do we hope to remove the scaffolding from our students' learning. Anything we want them to learn—how to solve problems, think through calculations, ask good questions, listen to and critique ideas—might initially require scaffolds. But our job as educators is not complete until we see students do these things without our direct intervention. When this happens, students have achieved autonomy.

Autonomy: *The ability to make choices and act on one's own free will.*

> Why Autonomy Matters

Instead of answering questions to please a teacher or earn a score—what psychologists refer to as *extrinsic* motivation—autonomy is a sign of an internally driven desire to learn—*intrinsic* motivation. When students' participation is internally driven by their curiosity and questions, it changes how they learn. Students are doing things to satisfy their own needs, pursuing their own interests and values to participate in our shared world, which Maxine Greene says is the essence of teaching. When they develop autonomy in their learning, it relates to a number of positive long-term outcomes. They are more likely to stay in school, pursue conceptual learning, seek out challenging work, and show more interest and enjoyment in their academic pursuits. (See Vallerand, Fortier, and Guay 1997; Vansteenkiste et al. 2004; Boggiano et al. 1988; Ryan and Connell 1989.)

How Autonomy Shifts Social Risk

Students assess the social risk of classroom situations by weighing the potential risks against the possible benefits. When students act autonomously in the classroom, the benefits of engagement are clear: they are pursuing their interests and ideas, garnering the inherent rewards of their activity. The optimal state of enjoyment and a sense of purpose—what psychologist Mihaly Csikszentmihalyi (1997) calls *flow*—is the ultimate manifestation of intrinsic motivation, where social risk recedes into the background and activity is autonomously driven. Although no teacher expects students to achieve this all the time, the long-term dividends of even occasionally having such a positively autonomous experience cannot be overstated. If students know that this enjoyable state can be achieved when learning math, then they are more willing to hang around in between these times. Equally important for intrinsic motivation are the aha! moments of discovery. When students only engage in mathematics by following somebody else's steps, they miss the opportunities to develop their own insights, along with the satisfaction that they bring.

This is not to say that teachers should provide students with complete autonomy. As teachers, we are obligated, to varying degrees in schools, to adhere to a curriculum, connected to courses and postsecondary education after students leave our classroom. Complete autonomy would not support these paths and could foreclose students' opportunities. Additionally, students need guidance on how to act autonomously. Routines, structures, and accountability systems help them *learn how to learn* productively, while being good citizens of our classrooms. They also give students permission to engage—to geek out and act with enthusiasm—something they may not be used to in school.

>> What Gets in the Way of Autonomy

As with belongingness, meaningfulness, competence, and accountability, many of the taken-for-granted aspects of school interfere with autonomy. Especially at larger schools, students can go through their days and not feel connected to what they are learning. They do not experience the belongingness that would give them the freedom to pursue their questions at school. In fact, in the traditional curriculum, students have few opportunities to engage personal interests—especially in math class. This suppresses autonomy in students' learning. Additionally, narrow ideas about competence can leave students feeling helpless if their particular strengths do not come into play in their schoolwork. Finally, schools often operate with a high degree of control over students' bodies (what they should wear, where they should sit, how they should walk, when they can use the bathroom) and minds (what they should be thinking about, how much time they should spend learning something). These coercive structures allow schools to manage crowds of children in small spaces, but they do not provide students with the sense of agency that leads to autonomy.

If students' cooperation in school is consistently sought out through coercive means, then they do not have opportunities to develop autonomy. Coercive systems provide extrinsic motivation for students' participation and engagement, making these behaviors a performance. Many classrooms use behavioral reward systems to foster participation. No doubt, the line between reward systems and scaffolds can be blurry. Sometimes we need to jump-start desired behaviors through reward systems. Only when the reward systems fade as students learn to act in desired ways are they truly scaffolds. If they remain in place and have no room to fade, then they are simply coercive and do not give students a chance to develop autonomy.

>> Strategies for Developing Students' Autonomy

When I asked the featured teachers how they knew when their teaching was going well, they all told stories about students acting autonomously. Clearly, the structures they provide are genuine scaffolds, meant to be taken up by students to guide independent learning. When students use them effectively without direct teacher supervision, the teachers know they have achieved an important goal: their students have learned how to learn mathematics together. The teachers help students develop autonomy by setting up environments that support student independence, through the use of noncontrolling language and by decentering themselves in the classroom.

Ideas from the #MTBoS

Helping Kids Find the Math They Love

Justin Lanier, Paul Salomon, and Anna Weltman curate a blog called *Math Munch* (mathmunch.org), a digest of math on the Internet. They share cool things people are doing with math, in the hopes of helping students find the math that they love. As Justin explained, "If a student can find one thing in math that they like—one thing in math that means something to them and that they succeed at—then they can't get away with saying 'I hate math' or 'I'm bad at math.' They may not like *all* math, but no one does. They may not be good at *all* math, but no one is. Having different tastes and talents is what makes each of us unique." Just as a good librarian can match students with the kinds of books they like, a rich buffet of mathematical bites can help students find their own mathematical preferences.

Environments for Student Independence

All of the featured teachers work to support students' autonomy. As should be clear by now, the various routines and structures allow for, among other things, student independence from direct teacher control by providing expectations and guidelines for students to follow. At Elizabeth Statmore's school, many students come from home cultures where direct discussions are not common, so she is aware of how Talking Points scaffold what may be novel forms of interaction. As she explained:

> *Many people are eye-shy. There are even some cultures in which they have been taught it's rude to look someone directly in the eye. But that's a huge part of American business culture. So learning how to bridge that cultural gap is important, because we want them to be empowered to make choices about code-switching.*

"Code-switching" refers to how people alternate between two or more forms of speech and communication. For Elizabeth's students, Talking Points provide a tool to support autonomy as they integrate home and school cultures. She sees her students use the Talking Points sheets as a prop as they develop communicative proficiency, something to look down at and make notes on. The expectations to share and listen are the same, but some the need for direct interaction is eased through her adaptation of the structure.

Interactions

The press for student independence also came through in how the teachers interacted with students around mathematics. In line with the meaningful mathematics they worked toward, the teachers expected students to contribute to conversations or change their minds based on their own understandings. Rafranz Davis consistently directed students away from answer getting toward sense making. She would point-blank ask them, "Tell me what this means to you," positioning the students as the owners of their mathematical thinking. Often, when students started to focus on meaning, she found they no longer needed her help. The metacognitive act of getting them to reflect on their own processes was enough to get them back on track.

Peg Cagle has routines during the sense-making parts of her lesson aimed at maximizing students' opportunities to think. For instance, during group work, she often directs students to have ten minutes of talk time, followed by two minutes of silent thinking. In this way, she honors the different ways her students might process the challenging questions she poses, giving everybody a chance to understand the problem situations.

When Fawn Nguyen guides student discussions in whole class or small groups, she often uses *revoicing* moves: restating another person's idea either to clarify it or connect it to other parts of the conversation. (See O'Connor and Michaels 1993.) The clarifying move is useful when students are figuring out a problem and their explanations are not entirely cogent. This might sound like, "So what I hear you saying is that zero is an even number?" It can also cast a rough draft contribution in academic language ("So you showed with your hand that the slope will go down. We call that 'decreasing.'"). By posing the restatement as a question, the original speaker has a chance to clarify, extend, or revise what the teacher says. The connecting move is useful when a student hits on an important idea and the teacher wants to make sure that other students have followed ("Clara, can you summarize what Samir just said?") or link it to other contributions ("Do I hear you saying that you think the lines intersect? Because earlier Taylor said they wouldn't."). These various revoicing moves emphasize the students' ownership of their thinking.

The Physical Environment

In addition to pressing for independent sense making, many of the teachers deliberately designed their rooms to allow students some free movement. As Elizabeth Statmore described, "I have my seating charts over by the self-serve table that has the supplies, and kids are always free to get up and get what they need." As students investigate statements during Talking Points, they have access to a variety of resources—rulers, calculators, compasses, patty paper—that will help them with their thinking. Giving students opportunities for free movement also helps them self-regulate if they need to move around and clear their head or take a break from a challenging situation.

Noncontrolling Language

In Fawn's room, "Don't let others think for you" is a mantra. The mantra targets the same desired behavior emphasized in Peg's classroom through her posters: "Ask, Don't Tell" and "Ask a good question and everybody starts thinking. Answer it and almost everybody stops." Both teachers want to shift students away from unproductive habits such as telling their peers answers without sense making or justification. Instead of simply sanctioning such behavior through demerits or scolding, the teachers focus on the consequences of their expectations on students' learning and well-being. Fawn reminds her students that they "want to make wise decisions. When you just go along with other people, you're not going to learn anything." This appeals to adolescents' emerging desire for autonomy beyond the classroom.

When students have negative experiences with structures and systems, the teachers listen nonjudgmentally, respectfully providing information for their classroom designs. When students balk at Peg not giving them answers during lessons, she has a clear response:

> I remind them about where we started, that there are other ways to do school. There are other ways to be the teacher and be in charge. I say that I don't want to do that. I don't—not because I don't like to, not because I don't think I can—but because I don't think it's ultimately the most productive place for them to learn. I let them know that what I care about, number one, is that my students all have the best shot at learning to their capacity in my classroom. That means that I can't be doing things that get in the way, and I can't let students do things that get in the way for other people.

Peg's response acknowledges what is hard about the new social contract for learning math in her classroom while emphasizing her care for them and her respect for their learning. Her system may challenge their well-developed habits, but it also gives them a freedom and respect that they could grow to appreciate.

Decentering Themselves in the Classroom

The featured teachers seek opportunities to decenter themselves from the class discussions. Over time, the norms, routines, and structures they have set up allow students to have productive mathematical discussions without their orchestration. Like all good scaffolds, they start to fade away. As Chris Luzniak describes:

> *A good discussion in my classroom involves students saying, "My claim is factoring is the best way to do this, and my warrant is. . . ." So using those types of structures is an important part. What would make a really good discussion is if they're listening and responding to each other, rather than just waiting to be called on to share an idea. Waiting to be called on to share an idea is how the year starts and then I really push different ways to have them listen to each other so I can just sit. Like, I sit down so I'm not even a focal point, and they're physically looking at each other, listening to each other, and coming to some kind of consensus or sharing different ideas and different approaches.*

Once his students take ownership of the Math Debate's claim and warrant structure, along with listening to each other's arguments, the discussions can proceed with students directly addressing each other and him on the side.

Similarly, Peg Cagle presses on her students' ownership of their mathematical thinking by striving to "never say anything a student can say." She emphasizes *questioning* in her interactions, working to draw out students' thinking instead of telling them the mathematics. Her students learn to dig deep into their group's resources before trying to solicit her help:

> *In groups, very often, kids ask me a question and I don't want to answer it. I rarely answer their questions. On my video for my Presidential [Award], on the audio track, as I'm walking away from group, in the background you can hear one kid say to another, "I told you there was no point in asking her. You know she's not going to answer us."*

She works hard to press students to use their own knowledge and thinking before they draw on hers. "My absolute pinnacle—and it doesn't happen often—is when I became just another participant" in the class discussions. She told me a story about a geometry class where a student popped out of her seat and ran to the front of the room to show something on the board. She said, "Here, Ms. Cagle, you can sit down," and proceeded with her explanation.

Although it is not always that dramatic, once students know how to talk about math together, the teacher's role shifts, even if it is temporary. Fawn sees this in her classroom too: "Some days, I just want to burst out in tears because they're so good." When she listens in on group work and hears students' thoughtful critiques of each other's ideas, she knows they have achieved something.

Similarly, Sadie Estrella sees scaffolds from her Counting Circles fall away over longer time periods (because she sees students throughout their high school years). By eleventh grade, her students are able to communicate about their learning in sophisticated ways. "They are better able to communicate, like, 'Oh, I don't know how to do this or these, this is where I'm getting stuck.'" Seeing her students become confident learners of math, knowing how to learn, is an important outcome in Sadie's classroom. When pressed and supported to talk about math independently, students can do it.

Autonomy Audit

1. What systems do you have in your classroom to get students to participate productively? To what extent are they coercive? To what extent do they allow students to make good choices?

2. What opportunities are there over the course of a year for students to enjoy mathematics? To have the pleasure of an aha! moment?

3. What structures do you have that might support students' development of independence in their mathematical work? How might you modify existing structures to better support this?

4. When students are reluctant to participate as you would like them to, how do you respond? Do you have informational and noncoercive ways of helping them understand your classroom?

5. Do the structures you put in place have a chance to fade away, giving students direct control over their mathematical sense making?

6. At what points in the year might you need to bring back your structures to reestablish norms (after vacation, learning challenging new content, when new students enter your class)? What are your strategies for doing so? How do you then let them fade again?

8 | Growing Your Own Practice

Educators need to reject the present methods fetish so as to create learning environments informed by both action and reflection. In freeing themselves from the blind adoption of so-called effective strategies, teachers can begin the reflective process, which allows them to recreate and reinvent teaching methods and materials by always taking into consideration the sociocultural realities that can either limit or expand the possibilities to humanize education.

—LILIA BARTOLOMÉ, "BEYOND THE METHODS FETISH: TOWARD A HUMANIZING PEDAGOGY"

Good teaching cannot be reduced to technique; good teaching comes from the identity and integrity of the teacher.

—PARKER PALMER, *THE COURAGE TO TEACH: EXPLORING THE INNER LANDSCAPE OF A TEACHER'S LIFE*

If you have made it to the final chapter of this book, you should have clearer images of motivational mathematics classrooms. I have shown how a variety of teachers in different settings lowered social risk for their students by fostering climates of belongingness, meaningfulness, competence, accountability, and autonomy. The following table summarizes the featured teachers' primary strategies for accomplishing this work. Through different routines, structures, and intentional relationship building, they increased the chances that students would participate willingly and productively in their math classrooms by lowering social risk.

Motivational Construct	Common Obstacles	Teachers' Strategies
Belongingness	• Students experience school as rejecting • Devaluing students' identities • Correcting the inconsequential • Having narrow ideas about "on-task" behavior	• Organizing physical space to welcome students • Routines and structures to orient students to activity • Advocating for students' inclusion in the classroom and in the school community
Meaningfulness	• Focusing on work production over ideas and connections • Rituals of compliance • Cue-based learning	• Setting up inviting problems • Making space for students' ideas • Finding problems together
Competence	• Emphasis on quick and accurate calculation over other kinds of mathematical thinking • Unchecked status dynamics that value students' social and academic ranking over the quality of their ideas	• Valuing different perspectives • Honoring challenges as a part of learning • Staying mindful of status threats
Accountability	• Relying on overly narrow evidence for learning • Using isomorphic pretests • Treaties between students and teachers that trade cooperation for minimal academic challenge	• Everyone participates • Focusing on ideas • Listening matters
Autonomy	• Limited opportunities for students to engage with their personal interests • Narrow ideas about competence that leave many students feeling undervalued and therefore less able to contribute • Coercive schooling structures that undermine student autonomy	• Making environments for student independence • Using noncontrolling language • Decentering yourself as teacher in the classroom

Strategies for Achieving a Motivational Classroom

As educators, we do not typically share instructional practice around a framework like this one. Instead, teachers usually seek help with one aspect of practice: using open-ended problems, leading discussions, or incorporating formative assessment. But, as Lilia Bartolomé (1994) cautions, the emphasis on methods sometimes leads teachers to miss the social and cultural realities of their students' lives and school settings as well as the larger purpose of any particular practice —the form/function distinction discussed in the introduction. What is more, we are the instruments of our teaching: our own selves—the cognitive, emotional, physical, and social beings that we are—shape what is possible for us to do and how we might possibly accomplish our goals. As Parker Palmer (1997) suggests, the authenticity of our teaching practice—the extent to which it is rooted in our selves—determines our work's integrity. I can no more say absolutely that a particular practice, detailed in all its glory, will work for you as a teacher with your classroom and students than I can predict the weather on a particular day two years from now. Both depend on numerous details about conditions to which I do not have access. However, I can talk about tendencies in classrooms, just as I can talk about how different atmospheric changes, land conditions, and types of climates make certain weather patterns more likely. (OK, I actually cannot do that. But somebody with more meteorological knowledge than I certainly could.)

Classroom motivational climates are the linchpin for all kinds of teacher improvement projects. These climates shape how students participate and what they are willing to do, which, in turn, changes the learning opportunities they have.

This vision for the classroom centers on *humanizing pedagogy*: approaches to teaching that acknowledge the humanity of both students and teachers. This approach moves beyond the particulars of methods to careful attention to the classroom (and school) as a learning environment. Teachers are not technicians who are better or worse at predetermined best practices. Instead, they are problem solvers who monitor the classroom climate, attend to the relationships and interactions among participants as activities unfold, identify what is working and diagnose what is not, and then draw on a rich repertoire of practices to tinker and adjust. That rich repertoire includes particular routines and practices, but, importantly, these routines and practices draw on the teachers' own strengths as they adapt them for their students. For instance, Sadie Estrella's Counting Circles may not be the right tool for Chris Luzniak's upper-level math courses, and Elizabeth Statmore's Talking Points require a certain level of English-reading fluency across students. (Though I would not be at all surprised if ingenious teachers found ways to adapt these routines to be meaningful for different student populations!)

In the rest of this chapter, I offer a guide to the teacher problem solving that supports humanizing pedagogy, drawing on the professional growth stories of the featured teachers and others I have worked with over the years.

> A Guide to Teacher Problem Solving

Classrooms are such complex and ever-changing places, teaching puzzles are endless. In fact, a good deal of my research focuses on how teachers solve problems together. I have watched and analyzed hundreds of hours of video of teachers talking together about their work, especially when they are trying to improve their practice.

Hopefully you have had a chance to work through some of the audit questions at the end of each chapter. You can also refer to the table at the start of this chapter to remember the key strategies the featured teachers used to foster motivation in their classrooms. Maybe these tools have helped you better diagnose some of the strengths and obstacles of your classroom learning environment. Maybe you already have some conjectures about how you can redesign things to shift students' risk-benefit calculus and increase their motivation to participate. Maybe this work has opened your eyes to broader improvement projects you want to engage in. This guide is designed to help you with that challenge. It identifies a sequence of actions you can take to identify and address your own personal classroom puzzles.

Know who you are as an educator.
Most of us enter the profession of teaching to make a difference in some way. To achieve the authenticity Parker Palmer describes, it is important to know who you are and your

particular purpose. For instance, Chris had two clear passions: mathematics and performance. He found a way to bring both of these strengths to his teaching. Fawn Nguyen's strength was a love of hard problems and a desire to use them with her students; Rafranz Davis observed students with acuity and used what she saw to build relationships; Sadie spoke the local Hawai'ian pidgin and could use this facility to connect with her students; and Peg Cagle had been professionally trained to design environments that supported productive use, something she could apply to her classroom. Elizabeth's identity as an educator was mission driven: she wanted to get more people of good character in the calculus pipeline. This goal has helped her evaluate where she is teaching, who her kindred spirits are, and how she wants to invest her energy. When she was not feeling professionally supported at one school, she moved to another school that was more aligned with her mission. Whatever they may be, try to identify your strengths and purpose as a math teacher so that you can work with clarity.

Identify a problem of practice, ideally one you can work on with a colleague.

I cannot emphasize this enough: the most productive teacher learning projects I have seen are goal driven. Goals allow you to focus your activities and identify resources that can help. Instead of saying simply, "I want to be a better math teacher," and attending every professional development opportunity that comes along, you can say, "I want to have a classroom where students share their thinking more frequently," or "I want to support immigrant students' participation in my classroom." These goals will help you search for and select the most meaningful opportunities.

One of Peg's goals in her early years of teaching was to reduce failure rates in algebra. She had a group of students who had flunked algebra repeatedly. This became a core problem for her work. Similarly, Sadie wanted to keep more of her students in the math pipeline—and in school. Fawn's goal stemmed directly from her strengths and purpose for teaching: she loved challenging math problems and wanted to share that love with her students.

Diagnose the root causes of that problem.

To work on your problem, you need to have a sense of where it comes from. Make some conjectures about what is going on in your learning environment. Brainstorm exhaustively and nonjudgmentally. Just keep asking yourself why this problem persists in your setting. You may even consider involving administrators, specialists in English language acquisition or special education, community members, or students themselves.

In fact, Peg used her struggling students as partners in making sense of the problem. They were brutally honest about why they did not succeed. To them, math did not make any sense. This, of course, is a problem of meaningfulness. Similarly, Sadie saw that her students had not yet developed fluency with math facts. She knew the community well and saw clearly how many of her students felt alienated from school. She worked on their competence and belongingness.

Ask what is in your scope of practice.

When you review your root causes list, there will surely be items that are outside of your control. Inevitably, teachers contend with problems that simply reflect broader social problems. Instead, hone in on root causes that you can address in your classroom, department, school, or community. Sadie could not rectify a number of the social problems her students contended with, but she could find ways to support their academic learning in her classroom. Filter down your list of conjectures to the ones you can address.

Make an action plan for addressing the problem, and be ready to revise it.

Once you have identified a focus problem and some workable conjectures about underlying causes, map out a plan. What are you going to do? As best as you can, name the steps. Draft a provisional timeline.

For her part, Peg worked on meaningfulness by designing opportunities for students to talk to each other. She soon realized that even though they started to explain their own thinking, they often did not listen to one another. Meaning does not happen from a monologue, so she revised her design to support them in listening to each other. Sadie searched for resources that would help her support her students' fluency while developing other mathematical competencies. She attended to their sense of belongingness by working intentionally on her relationships with them, making her care and support explicit.

Consider your resources.

Who will support you in your work? This can be colleagues, coaches, specialists, professional development providers, community members, or students. Principals and department heads can make a difference in supporting teachers' professional growth by providing resources, time, and space for this work. Additionally, they can guide you toward helpful initiatives in the district, region, or state while fending off demands that compete for your attention. If you find others addressing similar problems, inside or outside your own school, you have partners in the work. School-based partners know your students, administrators, and community, so they can help you problem solve from the inside. You can bounce ideas off each other, identify good resources and strategies, and troubleshoot when things get hard. In addition, all of the featured teachers engage with others online. Sometimes, they can identify others working on similar problems and then support each other over time.

What tools do you have? These can be textbooks, technology, movable desks, libraries, or math manipulatives. In the United States in particular, schools have vastly different resources. Some Parent Teacher Organizations raise tens of thousands of dollars annually, and teachers can apply for support. At most schools, teachers do not have this resource, but there might be Title I money or grants from district initiatives that can support your project.

Consider your limitations.

Teaching is such complex work. We all have things we can get better at. Take stock of your own personal strengths and weaknesses. Make sure your plan fits within what you have to offer. If you recognize some gaps in your own development, identify places for your own learning. Good professional development involves more than the one-shot workshop. It focuses on building content knowledge; organizes work around materials that can be used in the classroom; centers on specific instructional practices; has coherence; and garners the support of teacher communities over time (Garet et al. 2001). Sometimes, really good professional development can connect you to your purpose more deeply. It may be hard for teachers outside major metropolitan areas to find these opportunities, but an increasing number of professional learning opportunities are available online.

Fawn and Peg found professional development on leading mathematical discussions to help them grow that part of their practice and support them in incorporating rich problems. For Chris, finding the debate-across-the-curriculum professional development program was pivotal in helping him connect his performance passion to his math teaching. Early in her teaching career, Elizabeth realized she needed to relearn mathematics she never felt she understood, so she enrolled in classes to help strengthen her knowledge. She found the experience enriching, because, in addition to the content review, it allowed her to remember what students' frequently experience when they do not understand.

Work regularly on your problem; be persistent, yet patient.

Find a way to hold yourself accountable to your goals. Some really great teacher-change projects die out because people lose patience with the slow rate of change, encounter too

Modeling Lifelong Teacher Learning

Rafranz Davis is a model for lifelong teacher learning. She knew she wanted to teach in a way that centered on students and that building relationships was key to that. Her mother's example of deep relational work showed the possibilities for student belongingness, especially for African American students. Early in her teaching career, Rafranz participated in a program with Dr. Evelyn Boyd Granville, one of the first African American women to earn a PhD in mathematics. Dr. Granville developed elementary school enrichment programs, and Rafranz worked with her program for four years. Aside from being an important role model for Rafranz, Dr. Granville led a middle school Algebra Camp. She modeled leading discussions, sharing her practice with the teachers. "It was really about having [students] focus on the thinking." Having such an accomplished mathematician and educator as a mentor contributed to Rafranz's development. This was just the beginning of Rafranz's exploration of ways to make math meaningful to her students. Rafranz continues to be a passionate learner, leading efforts to meaningfully integrate technology in her school district.

many obstacles, or just lose focus because of all the other demands on their time. A (revisable) timeline can help foster your patience, because it reminds you that all of the change will not happen overnight. Think about identifying milestones along the way. You and your partners, whether in person or virtual, can help each other note the tiny signs of progress, troubleshoot the obstacles, and celebrate the big successes. Elizabeth refined Talking Points over several school years, and Sadie continually refined her approach to Counting Circles. She changed things yet again as a classroom coach, working with other teachers.

As you learn, share what you know. Stay open to new ideas.

Part of growing as an educator comes from finding new questions. In recent years, Peg has invested a lot of thought in designing meaningful formative assessments for her students. After attending numerous workshops and reading extensively on the topic, she began presenting on the topic at conferences.

Equally important, we need to recognize when a strategy has reached its limit. As Rafranz (2015) describes on her blog:

> There was a time in my academic career that I thought that every classroom should have an interactive whiteboard. As a matter of fact, I was my school district's in-house "expert" on all things SMART. I trained every teacher in our district at some point and even conducted outside trainings and conferences. I had clickers, a slate and a mindset that I could not and would not teach in a classroom without it.
>
> And then . . . everything changed . . .
>
> 1. The iPad released and my school bought some.
> 2. I found Twitter, Edcamp and connected to teachers.
> 3. I changed the way that I taught a little bit at a time.
>
> It was as if the walls of my classroom crumbled and everything that I thought about student engagement shifted. I wanted students to have more "hands-on" contact . . . not "drag and drop" technology, but to create beyond presentations. All of a sudden, it mattered that their work contained their own questions and research . . . their voice. It mattered that we didn't go to a lab for access but that kids had access when needed.

As Rafranz's ideas about teaching changed, her goals for using digital tools changed as well. She attributes her ongoing growth to the connections—both real and virtual—that she has with other educators who challenge and enrich her thinking. "This is why connectedness is a part of this work. You are different because you have no choice but to be. Curating and sharing implies that you want to support the learning of others. Contributing your own work to the academic space shows that you are willing to share your own practice." Curating and sharing your learning not only allows you to solidify your own growth, but allows you to learn from other teachers asking similar questions.

I invite you to share your growth with me and with the educators featured in this book. You can find us at:

Peg Cagle @pegcagle

Rafranz Davis @rafranzdavis

http://rafranzdavis.com/

Sadie Estrella @wahedahbug

http://iamamathnerd.wordpress.com

Ilana Horn @ilana_horn

https://teachingmathculture.wordpress.com

Chris Luzniak @PIspeak

https://clopendebate.wordpress.com/

Fawn Nguyen @fawnpnguyen

http://fawnnguyen.com, http://visualpatterns.org, http://mathtalks.net

Elizabeth Statmore @cheesemonkeysf

http://cheesemonkeysf.blogspot.com/

Stay connected to what you love, always.

Fawn attributes the longevity of her career to the love she feels in the classroom. She posted a thank-you note from a student on her blog:

Dear Ms. Nguyen,

Thank you so much for being such an outstanding teacher! I love coming into your classroom every day to learn about math in the most fun and engaging way possible. Day after day, you make me struggle with interesting and creative math problems that I just can't get enough of! Their difficulty makes them so much more rewarding when I finally solve them! Once again, thank you for being THE BEST MATH TEACHER EVER!!! (Nguyen 2016)

Although her 401(k) is not where she wants it to be, notes like this let her know she is meeting her goals as a teacher—and making a difference in students' lives.

> Moving Forward

As you work to create a motivational math classroom for yourself and your own students, I urge you to consider your students' experiences and imagine the extent to which they belong, find the work meaningful, and have opportunities to be competent; how you hold them accountable; and whether they have a chance to develop autonomy in their learning. I hope that you can use these chapters to tinker, problem solve, and build on your own strengths and the strengths of your students. Making our classrooms places where all of us, teachers and students, can grow and thrive would be a tremendous accomplishment.

Appendix: Resources for Problems and Practices

Following is a collection of resources that can help you deepen the mathematical conversations in your classroom. They come from teachers, educational researchers, and mathematicians.

> Which One Doesn't Belong? is a website dedicated to providing thought-provoking puzzles for math teachers and students alike. There are no answers provided as there are many different, correct ways of choosing which one doesn't belong.
>
> http://wodb.ca/

Mathematician James Tanton presents a whole host of curriculum essays, more general mathematical essays, and puzzlers. He offers books that address high school curriculum in a joyful and accessible way (with no sacrifice to rigor), respectful of the beauty and wondrous creative nature of mathematics.

http://www.jamestanton.com/

Educational technology coach and mathematics teacher John Stevens curates examples of "Would you rather . . .?" questions that inspire mathematical exploration.

http://www.wouldyourathermath.com/

Mathematics educator Andrew Stadel collects interesting estimation challenges designed to help improve students' number sense and problem solving skills.

http://www.estimation180.com/

Pyschologists Jon R. Star, Bethany Rittle-Johnson, and Kristie J. Newton have collected contrasting cases of important mathematical ideas to support students' conceptual understanding.

http://scholar.harvard.edu/contrastingcases

The Mathematics Assessment Project helps teachers bring mathematical practices to their classrooms. The site includes materials such as tasks, scoring guides, and videos to illustrate how they play out in classrooms.

http://map.mathshell.org/

NRICH is a team of teachers who strive for rich mathematical thinking. The site offers problems, articles, and games organized by grade level.

http://nrich.maths.org/frontpage

Illustrative Mathematics offers carefully vetted resources for teachers and teacher leaders to help support meaningful mathematical learning. The site offers rich, standards-based curricular materials.

https://www.illustrativemathematics.org/

The free Accountable Talk® Sourcebook is an extensive introduction to the purposes of Accountable Talk and the classroom practices that promote Accountable Talk discussions at all grade levels.

http://ifl.pitt.edu/index.php/educator_resources/accountable_talk

Math Munch is a weekly digest of the mathematical Internet, curated by Justin Lanier, Paul Salomon, and Anna Weltman. There is a guide for teachers to help with classroom use.

https://mathmunch.org/

The Educational Development Center has compiled these helpful tools for reflecting on and implementing accessibility strategies for mathematics classrooms.

http://www2.edc.org/accessmath/resources/strategies.asp

Youcubed is the brainchild of mathematics education researcher Jo Boaler. There are many resources on the site, including an archive of low floor/high ceiling tasks labeled by topic and grade level.

https://www.youcubed.org/grade/low-floor-high-ceiling/

REFERENCES

Armstrong, Thomas. 2012. *Neurodiversity in the Classroom: Strength-Based Strategies to Help Students with Special Needs Succeed in School and Life.* Alexandria, VA: ASCD.

Bartolomé, Lilia. 1994. "Beyond the Methods Fetish: Toward a Humanizing Pedagogy." *Harvard Educational Review* 64 (2): 173–95.

Boaler, Jo. 2002. *Experiencing School Mathematics: Traditional and Reform Approaches to Teaching and Their Impact on Student Learning.* Mawah, NJ: Lawrence Erlbaum Associates.

Boggiano, Ann K., et al. 1988. "Children's Preference for Challenge: The Role of Perceived Competence and Control." *Journal of Personality and Social Psychology* 54 (1): 134.

Booker, K. C., and J. H. Lim. 2016. "Belongingness and Pedagogy Engaging African American Girls in Middle School Mathematics." *Youth & Society* 0044118X16652757.

Brodesky, Amy, Caroline Parker, Elizabeth Murray, and Lauren Katzman. 2002. "Accessibility Strategies Toolkit for Mathematics." http://www2.edc.org/accessmath/resources /strategiesToolkit.pdf.

Cardone, Tina. 2013. *Nix the Tricks: A Guide to Avoiding Shortcuts that Cut Out Math Concept Development.* CreateSpace Independent Publishing Platform.

Cantor, Georg. 1867. *De aequationibus secundi gradus indeterminatis.* Doctoral thesis: University of Berlin.

Cohen, Elizabeth, and Rachel Lotan. 2014. *Designing Groupwork: Strategies for the Heterogeneous Classroom.* Third Edition. New York: Teachers College Press.

Csikszentmihalyi, Mihaly. 1997. *Finding Flow: The Psychology of Engagement with Everyday Life*. New York: Basic Books.

Davis, Rafranz. 2013. "Beyond the Tech to Engage the Disengaged." http://rafranzdavis .com/beyond-technology-engaging-the-disengaged/.

———. 2014a. "Math Talks with Braeden: Investigations Matter." http://rafranzdavis .com/math-talks-with-braeden-investigations-matter/.

———. 2014b. "Teaching to the Kids at the Back of the Room." Ignite talk from 2014 National Council of Supervisors of Mathematics. www.youtube.com/watch?v =DbROpxHtEGk.

———. 2015a. "Confessions of a Digital Leader: Connectedness Is a Part of This Work." http://rafranzdavis.com/confessions-of-a-digital-leader-connectedness-is-a-part -of-this-work/.

———. 2015b. *The Missing Voices in EdTech: Bringing Diversity into EdTech*. Thousand Oaks, CA: Corwin Press.

Doyle, Walter. 1988. "Work in Mathematics Classes: The Context of Students' Thinking During Instruction." *Educational Psychologist* 23 (2): 167–80.

Emdin, Christopher. 2016. *For White Folks Who Teach in the Hood . . . and the Rest of Y'all Too: Reality Pedagogy and Urban Education*. Boston: Beacon Press.

Engle, R. A., and F. R. Conant. 2002. "Guiding Principles for Fostering Productive Disciplinary Engagement: Explaining an Emergent Argument in a Community of Learners Classroom." *Cognition and Instruction* 20 (4): 399–483.

Fielding, Michael. 2001. "Students as Radical Agents of Change." *Journal of Educational Change* 2 (2): 123–41.

Furrer, Carrie, and Ellen Skinner. 2003. "Sense of Relatedness as a Factor in Children's Academic Engagement and Performance." *Journal of Educational Psychology* 95 (1): 148.

Garet, Michael S., et al. 2001. "What Makes Professional Development Effective? Results from a National Sample of Teachers." *American Educational Research Journal* 38 (4): 915–45.

Gehlbach, Hunter, et al. 2012. "Changes in Teacher–Student Relationships." *British Journal of Educational Psychology* 82: 690–704.

Gehlbach, Hunter, et al. 2016. "Creating Birds of Similar Feathers: Leveraging Similarity to Improve Teacher–Student Relationships and Academic Achievement." *Journal of Educational Psychology* 108 (3): 342.

Greene, Maxine. 1987. Commencement Address, Bank Street College of Education, New York City.

Gutiérrez, Rochelle. 1996. "Practices, Beliefs and Cultures of High School Mathematics Departments: Understanding Their Influence on Student Advancement." *Journal of Curriculum Studies* 28 (5): 495–529.

———. 2013. "The Sociopolitical Turn in Mathematics Education." *Journal for Research in Mathematics Education* 44 (1): 37–68.

Herzig, A. H. 2002. "Where Have All the Students Gone? Participation of Doctoral Students in Authentic Mathematical Activity as a Necessary Condition for Persistence Toward the Ph.D." *Educational Studies in Mathematics* 50 (2): 177–212.

Horn, Ilana Seidel. 2008. "Turnaround Students in High School Mathematics: Constructing Identities of Competence Through Mathematical Worlds." *Mathematical Thinking and Learning* 10 (3): 201–39.

———. 2012. *Strength in Numbers: Collaborative Learning in Secondary Mathematics.* Reston, VA: National Council of Teachers of Mathematics.

Institute for Learning. 2015. "Accountable Talk® Practices." http://ifl.pitt.edu/index.php /educator_resources/accountable_talk.

Kohli, Rita, and Daniel G. Solórzano. 2012. "Teachers, Please Learn Our Names! Racial Micro Aggressions and the K–12 Classroom." *Race Ethnicity and Education* 15 (4): 441–62.

Kumashiro, Kevin. 2012. "Anti-Oppressive Education." In *The Encyclopedia of Diversity in Education,* James A. Banks (Ed.). pp. 111–113. Thousand Oaks, CA: SAGE Publishing.

Lakatos, Imre. 2015. *Proofs and Refutations: The Logic of Mathematical Discovery.* Cambridge University Press.

Liljedahl, Peter. 2016. "Building Thinking Classrooms: Conditions for Problem Solving." In *Posing and Solving Mathematical Problems,* 361–86. Springer International Publishing.

Lortie, Dan Clement. 1975. *Schoolteacher: A Sociological Study.* Chicago: University of Chicago Press.

McGee, Ebony Omtola. 2016. "Devalued Black and Latino Racial Identities: A By-Product of STEM College Culture?" *American Educational Research Journal* 53 (6): 1626–62.

McGraw, Rebecca, Lubienski, Sarah, and Strutchens, Marilyn. 2006. "A Closer Look at Gender in NAEP Mathematics Achievement and Affect Data: Intersections with Achievement, Race/Ethnicity, and Socioeconomic Status." *Journal for Research in Mathematic Education* 37 (2): 129–50.

Meier, Deborah. 2002. *The Power of Their Ideas: Lessons for America from a Small School in Harlem.* Beacon Press.

Mercer, Neil, and Steve Hodgkinson, eds. 2008. *Exploring Talk in School: Inspired by the Work of Douglas Barnes.* Thousand Oaks, CA: SAGE Publications.

Mirzakhani, Maryam. 2014. "Maryam Mirzakhani: 'The More I Spent Time on Maths, the More Excited I Got.'" *The Guardian.* August 2014. Retrieved April 5, 2017. www.theguardian.com/science/2014/aug/13/interview-maryam-mirzakhani-fields-medal-winner-mathematician.

Moll, L. C., C. Amanti, D. Neff, and N. Gonzalez. 1992. "Funds of Knowledge for Teaching: Using a Qualitative Approach to Connect Homes and Classrooms." *Theory Into Practice* 31 (2), 132–41.

Montessori, Maria. 1949/1987. *The Absorbent Mind.* New York: Dell.

National Council of Teachers of Mathematics. n.d. "Ages of Three Children." *The Math Forum.* http://mathforum.org/library/drmath/view/58492.html.

Nguyen, Fawn. n.d. *Math Talks.* www.mathtalks.net/teachers.html.

———. 2014. "Four Square and Other Questions." http://fawnnguyen.com/four-square-and-other-questions/.

———. 2016. "Making a Difference." http://fawnnguyen.com/making-a-difference/.

Nolen, Susan B. 2011. "The Role of Educational Systems in the Link Between Formative Assessment and Motivation." *Theory into Practice* 50 (4): 319–26.

O'Connor, Mary Catherine, and Sarah Michaels. 1993. "Aligning Academic Task and Participation Status Through Revoicing: Analysis of a Classroom Discourse Strategy." *Anthropology and Education Quarterly* 24 (4): 318–35.

Paley, Vivian Gussin. 2000. *White Teacher.* Cambridge, MA: Harvard University Press.

Palmer, Parker J. 1997. *The Courage to Teach: Exploring the Inner Landscape of a Teacher's Life.* Hoboken, NJ: John Wiley & Sons.

Paulos, John Allen. 1991. *Beyond Numeracy.* New York: First Vintage Books.

Powell, Arthur G., Eleanor Farrar, and David K. Cohen. 1985. *The Shopping Mall High School.* Boston: Houghton Mifflin.

Ray, Max. 2013. *Powerful Problem Solving: Activities for Sense Making with the Mathematical Practices.* Portsmouth, NH: Heinemann.

Ritchhart, Ron. 2015. *Creating Cultures of Thinking: The 8 Forces We Must Master to Truly Transform Our Schools.* Hoboken, NJ: John Wiley & Sons.

Ryan, Richard M., and James P. Connell. 1989. "Perceived Locus of Causality and Internalization: Examining Reasons for Acting in Two Domains." *Journal of Personality and Social Psychology* 57 (5): 749.

Schoenfeld, Alan H. 1988. "When Good Teaching Leads to Bad Results: The Disasters of 'Well-Taught' Mathematics Courses." *Educational Psychologist* 23 (2): 145–66.

Selling, Sarah Kate. 2016. "Making Mathematical Practices Explicit in Urban Middle and High School Mathematics Classrooms." *Journal for Research in Mathematics Education* 47 (5): 505–51.

Sengupta-Irving, Tesha, and Noel Enyedy. 2014. "Why Engaging in Mathematical Practices May Explain Stronger Outcomes in Affect and Engagement: Comparing Student-Driven with Highly Guided Inquiry." *Journal of the Learning Sciences* 24 (4): 550–92.

Shell Centre. n.d. "Mathematics Assessment Project: Assessing 21st Century Math." Accessed April 5, 2017 http://map.mathshell.org/lessons.php.

Shumway, Jessica. 2011. *Number Sense Routines: Building Numerical Literacy Every Day in Grades K–3.* Portland, ME: Stenhouse.

Stafford, Will. 2016. "Create Debate." Paper presented at NCTM San Francisco 2016, San Francisco, CA. https://nctm.confex.com/nctm/2016AM/webprogram/Handout /Session41215/Create%20Debate%20Final.pdf.

Steele, Claude M., and Joshua Aronson. 1995. "Stereotype Threat and the Intellectual Test Performance of African Americans." *Journal of Personality and Social Psychology* 69 (5): 797.

Stein, Mary Kay, and Margaret Schwan Smith. 2011. *5 Practices for Orchestrating Productive Mathematics Discussions.* Reston, VA: National Council of Teachers of Mathematics.

Stenmark, Jean Kerr. 1991. *Mathematics Assessment: Myths, Models, Good Questions, and Practical Suggestions.* Reston, VA: National Council of Teachers of Mathematics.

Stiggins, Rick, and Jan Chappuis. 2005. "Using Student-Involved Classroom Assessment to Close Achievement Gaps." *Theory into Practice* 44 (1): 11–8.

Stigler, James W., and James Hiebert. 2009. *The Teaching Gap: Best Ideas from the World's Teachers for Improving Education in the Classroom.* New York: Simon and Schuster.

Stipek, Deborah, et al. 1998. "The Value (and Convergence) of Practices Suggested by Motivation Research and Promoted by Mathematics Education Reformers." *Journal for Research in Mathematics Education* 29 (4): 465–88.

Thanheiser, Eva, and Amanda Jansen. 2016. "Inviting Prospective Teachers to Share Rough Draft Mathematical Thinking." *Mathematics Teacher Educator,* 4 (2): 145–63.

Third International Mathematics and Science Study. n.d. "US87 (From TIMSS 1995 Video Study)." *TIMSS Video.* Accessed April 5, 2017 at http://www.timssvideo.com/97.

Tobias, Sheila. 1990. *They're Not Dumb, They're Different—Stalking the Second Tier.* Tucson, AZ: Research Corporation.

Turner, Julianne C., et al. 2014. "Enhancing Students' Engagement: Report of a 3-Year Intervention with Middle School Teachers." *American Educational Research Journal* 51 (6): 1195–1226.

Vallerand, Robert J., Michelle S. Fortier, and Frédéric Guay. 1997. "Self-Determination and Persistence in a Real-Life Setting: Toward a Motivational Model of High School Dropout." *Journal of Personality and Social Psychology* 72 (5): 1161.

Vansteenkiste, Maarten, et al. 2004. "Motivating Learning, Performance, and Persistence: The Synergistic Effects of Intrinsic Goal Contents and Autonomy-Supportive Contexts." *Journal of Personality and Social Psychology* 87 (2): 246.

Wigfield, Allan, and Jacquelynne Eccles, eds. 2002. "The Development of Competence Beliefs and Values from Childhood Through Adolescence." In *Development of Achievement Motivation*. Hoboken, NJ: John Wiley & Sons.

Wiliam, Dylan. 2011. *Embedded Formative Assessment.* Bloomington, IN: Solution Tree Press.

Wiliam, Dylan, and Siobhán Leahy. 2015. *Embedding Formative Assessment: Practical Techniques for K–12 Classrooms.* West Palm Beach, FL: Learning Sciences International.

Youcubed at Stanford University. 2016. "Tasks by Grade: Low Floor High Ceiling." www.youcubed.org/grade/low-floor-high-ceiling/.